P9-CMO-202

15,659

LB
1031   Dunn
.D8   Practical
           approaches to
           individualizing
           instruction

DATE DUE

Practical approaches to individualizing
LB1031.D8   15659

Dunn, Rita Stafford 1930-
        VRJC/WRIGHT LIBRARY

Practical Approaches to Individualizing Instruction:

Contracts and Other Effective Teaching Strategies

Practical Approaches to Individualizing Instruction:

Contracts and Other Effective Teaching Strategies

Rita Dunn

Kenneth Dunn

Parker Publishing Company, Inc.
West Nyack, New York

VERNON REGIONAL
JUNIOR COLLEGE LIBRARY

© 1972, *by*

PARKER PUBLISHING COMPANY, INC.
West Nyack, N.Y.

*All rights reserved. No part of this book
may be reproduced in any form or by any
means, without permission in writing from
the publisher.*

Library of Congress Cataloging in Publication Data

Dunn, Rita Stafford, Date
    Practical approaches to individualizing instruction.

    Bibliography: p.
    1. Individualized instruction. 2. Education--Ex-
perimental methods. I. Dunn, Kenneth J., joint author.
II. Title.
LB1031.D8   371.39'4   72-3219
ISBN 0-13-687103-8

Printed in the United States of America

With Individual and Collective Love,
to Keith, Kevin, Kerry, Ricky, Rana and Robert

Also by One of the Authors

Using Instructional Media Effectively,
Jack Tanzman and Kenneth J. Dunn,
Parker Publishing Company, Inc., 1971.

Foreword

FABLE OF THE ACTIVITY CURRICULUM, OR THE DIFFERENCES IN
INDIVIDUAL DIFFERENCES

By Dr. G. H. Reavis (deceased June 12, 1970), outstanding educator and founder of the Phi Delta Kappa Educational Foundation.

Once upon a time, the animals decided they must do something to meet the problems of "the new world," so they organized a school. They adopted an activity curriculum consisting of running, climbing, swimming and flying, and, to make it easier to administer, all the animals took all subjects.

The duck was an excellent student in swimming, better in fact than the instructor, and made passing grades in flying, but he was very poor in running. Since he was slow in running, he had to stay after school and also drop swimming to practice running. This was kept up until his web feet were badly worn and he was only average in swimming. But average was acceptable in school, so nobody worried about that except the duck.

The rabbit started at the top of the class in running, but had a nervous breakdown because of so much makeup work in swimming.

The squirrel was excellent in climbing until he developed frustration in the flying class where his teacher made him start from the ground up, instead of from the treetop down. He also developed charlie horses from overexertion and then got C in climbing and D in running.

The eagle was a problem child and was disciplined severely. In climbing class he beat all others to the top of the tree, but insisted on using his own way to get there.

At the end of the year, an abnormal eel that could swim exceedingly well, and also run, climb and fly a little had the highest average and was valedictorian.

* * * * *

This famous fable, written more than 20 years ago, neatly destroys the prescribed curriculum and casts much doubt on some elements of the instruc-

7

tional process. To require all children to pass through "4th grade" while learning the same subjects at the same time with the identical degree of expected proficiency, denies individual differences among children just as surely as the Fable's activity curriculum forced the duck to run and the rabbit to swim—by the end of the school year!

The detrimental requirements for the poor animals in the Fable were not very different from those forced on many of our students whose strengths and interests are ignored and whose weaknesses are "hung 'round their necks" like another fabled animal, the albatross.

R. D.
K. D.

The Objectives of This Book

This book offers a variety of effective ways to individualize instruction in the classroom. "Contracts" offer an especially practical and organized method of reaching this goal. The many techniques described in Chapters 3, 6, 7 and 8 may be used by teachers who wish to begin the individualization process slowly, and may be incorporated into the contract approach as confidence and skill develop.

The use of contracts may be traced back to 1915 and early "laboratory" plans. At that time contracts consisted of units or work projects that involved readings, exercises and written assignments to be completed in a specified amount of time, usually three or four weeks.

Recently, various programs intended to permit individual rather than group pacing [e.g., Individually Prescribed Instruction (IPI), Program for Learning in Accordance with Needs (Project Plan), Teaching Learning Units (TLUs) and Learning Activity Packages (LAPs)] have taken advantage of what we now know about the inability of all children to progress at the same rate of speed while learning. These attempts at individualizing instruction do provide opportunities for students to proceed at different rates, but sequenced packages are not designed to include student interaction, peer sharing, small-group techniques and independently designed learning contracts.

The curriculum and independent contracts in this book blend the best of the original contract concept and the newer, more individualized programs into a stimulating and useful approach to meeting the needs of all students, from slow learners to those with more advanced skills and abilities. Moreover, these contracts provide alternate ways of learning, optional media resources and varied group activities, as well as several patterns of developing student and teacher objectives and progress evaluations.

The book takes the teacher (and administrator) through the step-by-step development of contracts in phases, and details several effective instructional techniques that can be put into practice quickly and easily. Small-group strategies as well as personalized prescriptions are provided to remove the lonely and often alienating environment that frequently characterizes the sequenced curriculum package. Moreover, the ideas, lessons and materials described in this book *have been tried and proven successful* at all levels, from the primary school through the university, and during in-service courses and professional institutes.

In addition to the many practical suggestions for varied and improved teaching strategies, teachers can add "learning stations, media corners, interest centers, little theaters, game tables, and magic carpets" to their classrooms with just a little organization and effort, within a few days.

For those teachers who are challenged by the seemingly impossible task of meeting each youngster's learning needs, a complete how-to-individualize program is described in Parts I and II. Various types of student contracts are presented and there are dozens of blueprints for action that can be tailored to any instructional situation. Teachers will be able to follow the guidelines for preparing contracts by using the materials and techniques already at their disposal through a structured framework for individualization that does not require countless hours of preparation time. Further, the continuing development of curriculum and independent contracts will provide a growing library of student media resources, activities and reporting alternatives, that will promote satisfying and relatively effortless individualization within a short period of time when compared to the usual year-after-year curriculum writing projects.

Each chapter in Part III develops one or more unique instructional methods and suggests teaching techniques and appropriate applications for students with different learning styles. Brainstorming, simulations, team learning, circles of knowledge and spheres of interest are among the practical strategies designed for effective instruction and student participation. These teaching strategies are described in full detail. Several ready-to-use samples are included and provide a perfect complement to individualized contracts.

This book was written in response to a need and to a challenge: a need for simple techniques to individualize instruction and a challenge to demonstrate that teaching and learning can be stimulating, enjoyable, relevant and appropriate to all students—whether "slow," "average" or "advanced"—for, in effect, these labels are false and do not recognize individual differences. Through the use of contracts, each child's program becomes individualized in relation to his needs, abilities and objectives. Indeed, the approach can eliminate failure of any type, and success can be made relevant to each child's progress on his own path to fulfillment.

Rita Dunn
Kenneth Dunn

Acknowledgments

With Special Thanks to
Margaret J. Reddy, Ruth Allen, Larry Scribnick
and Elaine Arnold

CONTENTS

Part II   Developing Contracts

Part III   Using Effective Teaching Strategies • 149

Practical Approaches to Individualizing Instruction:

Contracts and Other Effective Teaching Strategies

I

Individualizing
Instruction

1

Developing a Dynamic Program to Improve Teaching and Learning

Learning: Fallacies and Realities

Some schools operate daily instructional programs that are based on serious misconceptions about the learning process. Current teaching methods often *block* learning and promote a conformity that prevents the establishment of appropriate objectives for each student. It follows that drastic instructional and organizational change is needed to revise and improve the teaching-learning process. This type of sweeping change for the better can best begin through an understanding of the common fallacies and realities that now exist in our classrooms.

Fallacy #1: Children learn by listening.
Reality: Children may learn by listening, but are more likely to learn by talking, doing and *teaching.*

Learning rarely occurs by exposing passive listeners to "instructors" who possess and recite information. This tuning "out" instead of "in" occurs most often when a *group* is the recipient of a lecture. Learning requires active participation in the learning process; the learner must be *aggressively involved* in acquiring knowledge (Photo 1-1).

Despite this reality, most of our classes function in the reverse pattern—the *active* person (talking, demonstrating, moving, directing) is the *teacher.* The pupil (who should be actively involved and participating if he is to learn the things to which he has been exposed) is *passive.* In fact, the more quiet the pupil is, the more he is appreciated and praised by his teacher. For many years, educators erroneously equated passive conformity with "paying attention" and learning.

Photo 1-1. *Passive viewing and listening by medium-sized or large groups should be used only for introducing new concepts; individualized or small-group activity should dominate the learning environment. (Photograph courtesy of The Shaver Partnership, Architects, Salina, Kansas.)*

Youngsters often merely serve as an audience for teachers when they sit politely and listen to diatribes that essentially serve to reinforce the teacher's knowledge—not necessarily adding to the children's understandings, skills or abilities. It has been estimated that we can "think" about 400 words or more per minute as compared with the 100 or so words that are spoken by a lecturer in the same 60 seconds. It would seem to be an uneven instructional contest in favor of boredom, unless we allow the media-filled youngsters numerous opportunities to talk and teach!

Fallacy #2: A class of 25 or more children can learn identical content in a specific period of time.

Reality: Children learn different amounts of content at different rates at different times; they also vary in the amount they *retain.*

Most school districts follow "prescribed courses of study" for given grade or achievement levels, and each group is expected to complete the required curriculum between September, when school begins, and June, when the term officially ends. This procedure is ludicrous in view of the fact that our schools are in the business of mass education. Schools try to teach and enlighten every child, and, although teachers clearly recognize that children *are* drastically different from each other, they rarely act on this basic reality. Instead of building on the strengths and interests of each youngster, teachers often do what E.E. Cummings deplored—they try to make students "everybody else."

When children *want* to learn specific things, they absorb that knowledge easily and effortlessly, but when educators identify what children want to learn, they find that each child frequently wants to learn about something different. If they are to guide children into the learning process successfully, teachers must be free and sufficiently competent to prescribe those curriculum areas that are most interesting to the student. In this approach, children will be learning different things at different times. It is true that the totality of knowledge acquired by one youngster may never resemble what has been absorbed by another pupil in this system, but the achievement of each will promote greater understanding and ability to use what is learned.

We must stop believing that everyone needs to know and is capable of learning and retaining the same curriculum. The knowledge explosion and rapid social and technological change make "covering the curriculum" less and less appropriate. The pure content approach literally threatens our survival against overpopulation, pollution, violence and too-rapid technological advances by not teaching students how to solve problems and cope with the staggering rate of change.

Fallacy #3: Children can absorb the same content to the same depth.
Reality: Children can all learn *something* about a given topic, but each child has a greater or lesser capacity to absorb details, concepts and nuances of meaning. Here too, much of the result depends upon interest and an understanding of the frame of reference of each youngster.

If we believe that there are certain curriculum areas that are absolutely necessary for every child, let us rationally identify that which constitutes the minimum learning essentials in each area for every child. Let us then determine the additional facts that many children may be able and willing to learn in the selected area and offer that knowledge to those students. Teachers should recognize that each child cannot and need not learn everything that every other child does.

Fallacy #4: All children can learn if they will listen and "concentrate."

Reality: Each youngster has a unique learning style that may differ slightly or radically from that of his peers.

Depending upon their perceptual strengths (and weaknesses), some children learn by listening (auditory learners); some learn by seeing (visual learners); other children learn through touching (tactile learners) and still others learn through whole-body involvement (kinesthetic learners). *All children learn* when they are actively involved in the instructional process through their ears, eyes, touch and whole-body movements and responses, because these provide a multiple sensory approach to learning. Multiple sensory teaching techniques are likely to reach all youngsters and reveal individual learning styles.

Fallacy #5: A quiet school is a good school.

Reality: A quiet school is a subdued school, where children have been coerced into patterns of behavior that are unnatural to youth.

Healthy children are filled with curiosity, energy, loquacity and the need to interact with other people. A "good" school provides pupils with countless opportunities to explore an infinite variety of experiences. These learning activities should be followed by discussions, experiments and additional experiences that reinforce the students' newly gained understandings through socially acceptable classroom interaction that involves teaching and learning *noise*. "Quiet" classrooms are not conducive to experiences that permit a broad and frequent range of individual participations and are often the antithesis of a positive learning environment.

Fallacy #6: Children should be admitted to school when they become five years of age.

Reality: Children should be admitted to school when they are "ready" to learn.

Youngsters should be pretested by a school psychologist and observed by competent, experienced teachers in active class situations. In addition, the parents should be interviewed as part of the overall analysis. Depending upon the results of an objective team diagnosis, a student of any age should be admitted into either an informal or a structured program in accordance with his: (a) perceptual strengths and/or weaknesses, (b) motivational levels, (c) amount of self-discipline, (d) current interest areas and (e) achievement level in terms of ability to comprehend and follow instructions. In this system, some children would be "admitted" to a program at age three while others would not begin until age eight or nine.

Fallacy #7: It is better for children to remain on "grade level" with youngsters of the same chronological age rather than to work with either younger or older children.

Reality: It is better for children to be working at their maximum individual capacities with either similar or different age groups than to be bored by being unchallenged or frustrated because they are unable to compare themselves favorably with their peers.

All children should experience working with both younger and older children at times *if* they can work well together on similar achievement and interest levels. Grade levels should be eliminated entirely in favor of an essentially individualized program. Interaction among children of differing age or ability levels should be planned carefully to provide a social and academic climate that aids the learning process. Sharing, tutoring, group learning, project teams and cooperative task forces should be jointly designed and evaluated by students and teachers.

Fallacy #8: There are special teaching methods that are panaceas for instructing children; e.g., "discovery" in social studies, "phonics" in reading, "projects" in science, etc.

Reality: There is no single panacea that can offer every child (or most children) an easy way to learn a topic, content area or skill.

Because children learn in different ways, it is necessary to diagnose each child's perceptual strengths and then build into his learning program a variety of resource alternatives (books, films, slides, pictures, tapes, TV cassettes, etc.) through which he can learn. A repertoire of teaching methods is also essential if teachers are to discover every child's unique learning style.

Any school that discards one method in preference to another is probably a victim of the "bandwagon syndrome." No single approach can replace a variety of methods in each curriculum area. Even if some students' perceptual strengths and inclinations verify that they may lean heavily upon a particular method through which to acquire knowledge, the exposure to the same information through other available methods supplies the reinforcement, intensity and variety that are necessary to assure retention.

Fallacy #9: The teacher should be accountable for the child's learning.
Reality: The child should be accountable for his learning.

A teacher must be responsible for correctly diagnosing each child's strengths and weaknesses and prescribing what and how the student should learn. The instructor must then serve as a learning facilitator and prescriber of resources in the learning process. The teacher should not be "accountable," however, for anyone other than himself because motivation is personal and complex. A child can learn anything he wants—however, only he can will himself to *want* to learn. His home, his teacher, his school, his peers and his environment contribute to building (or diminishing) his motivation, but the individual child is the only one who can generate desire and motivation for his own learning. The teacher should be accountable, however, for the opportunities he provides and for his role in the successful diagnosis and prescription of learning styles and experiences.

Fallacy #10: A "great" teacher must be an excellent actor or actress.
Reality: A great teacher establishes rapport, respect and a climate that creates a personalized joy of learning and achieving for each of his students.

Even great actors and actresses find it difficult to compete successfully with life and television for children's sustained attention. Today's "great" teachers diagnose children accurately, prescribe in accordance with the child's abilities and interests, serve as positive guides and encourage each student to achieve to the maximum of his ability. The better teachers permit children to "do their own thing" and no longer compulsively require their captive audience to do theirs.

Fallacy #11: Young children need a "mother substitute" or "anchor." Therefore, the self-contained classroom, where one teacher is responsible for most of the learning for a group of children, is the best organizational pattern for primary grades.

Reality: Young children need a variety of challenging activities, and many require warm and responsive adults; other children need loving parents; others need opportunities to become independent and responsible.

Any organizational pattern that provides for children's needs will be effective. Obviously, it is not the specific organizational pattern, but what happens within each classroom and learning center that determines the quality of the educational experience afforded to each of the students involved.

There are, however, many interesting (and exciting) patterns that provide the increased flexibility, variety and individualization that are more conducive to a positive learning environment and the development of pupil responsibility than the self-contained classroom, but none of these have very much to do with the impossible (and unnecessary) task of providing children with substitutes for their mothers. Indeed, some "substitute mothers" might continue the overprotection that prevents independence: single "anchors" can weigh some children down or (at best) prevent them from forging ahead at full speed with other "skippers and sails."

Fallacy #12: Each teacher knows what is "best" for the children in her class.

Reality: Every teacher is not like every other teacher; some are excellent diagnosticians, some are effective prescribers, some are outstanding guides and some are excellent at all or none of these functions.

Teachers should have assignments that make the best use of their strengths, or they should be encouraged to "team" with other professionals who show ability in their areas of weakness. No one person should be solely responsible for the learning of any single child nor should a single teacher be expected to be an expert in all content areas or instructional functions.

Fallacy #13: Children learn best through repeated sequential periods that are spaced throughout the school day and year and are "articulated" with the same subjects in succeeding days and years.[1]

Reality: Children learn best through a variety of structured and unstructured approaches.

---

[1]Various organizational approaches have been devised for this purpose; e.g., vertical curriculum, spiral curriculum, continuous progress plan, core curriculum, dual progress plan, departmentalization, tract systems, integrated curriculum, etc.

Some youngsters respond best to short, concentrated "mini-courses," while others can study a single topic in depth for several semesters. Many students need "forgetting" periods after intensive study, while a few may thrive on continuing attention to a topic of interest. Even the "integrated day" should provide for these differences.

The ritual of repeating English or mathematics at the same time for the same period every day and then hitching the course or subject to another one is indefensible. Individual objectives and personalized learning should replace mindless scheduling according to the clock, bus arrivals, teacher load and other expedients that have nothing to do with learning.

Fallacy #14: Education takes place between the hours of 8:30 a.m. and 3:00 p.m. when children are in school.

Reality: Learning occurs whenever children are actively involved in stimulating experiences on their level of ability.

For many children, full days of schooling (8:30-3:00) are much too long; these students are not able to sustain interest or concentration for this length of time. There are some children, however, for whom the schools should be open on a 24-hours-a-day basis. These youngsters have a hunger and thirst for active learning that is apparently unquenchable. Children should be in school (or *learning*) for the periods of time during which they are capable of remaining motivated and self-disciplined, and not one minute more. The hours of school should, therefore, be flexible. School buildings and their human and physical resources should be available to children and adults in the community on a full-time basis for 24 hours a day. Residents should be able to come and go as they require guidance and assistance. Education might then reach the level of importance we have traditionally, but only verbally, ascribed to it.

Learning Styles:
The Need to Personalize Teaching

In addition to the traditional fallacies that schools continue to follow, there are errors of "omission" in current educational practice. Schools usually do not capitalize on existing knowledge of varying "learning styles." Each pupil is not diagnosed to determine the teaching strategies through which the youngster can learn best. As indicated earlier, perceptual testing is rarely employed to identify whether a student is a visual, phonetic, tactile or kinesthetic learner. In addition to this critical omission, children are rarely provided with the variety of media that would utilize the most effective learning style for each student.

The student, teacher and other members of the instructional team, such as aides, specialists or student teachers, should analyze and determine each youngster's learning style. Reassessment should be made from time to time to confirm the analysis and adjust for changes in mental growth, attitudes and interests. Each student works best under selected conditions and with certain combinations of multimedia resources and motivations.

These are some of the "style" elements which should be checked.

Learning Style Diagnosis

1. *Time*	(When is the student most alert? In the early morning, at lunch time, in the afternoon, in the evening, at night?)
2. *Schedule*	(What is the student's attention span? Continuous, irregular, short bursts of concentrated effort, forgetting periods, etc.?)
3. *Amount of Sound*	(What level of noise can the student tolerate? Absolute quiet, a murmur, distant sound, high levels of conversation?)
4. *Type of Sound*	(What type of sound produces a positive reaction? Music, conversation, laughter, working groups?)
5. *Type of Work Group*	(How does the student work best? Alone, with one person, with a small task group, in a large team, a combination?)
6. *Amount of Pressure*	(What kind of pressure [if any] does the student need? Relaxed, slight, moderate, extreme?)
7. *Type of Pressure and Motivation*	(What helps to motivate this student? Self, teacher expectation, deadlines, rewards, recognition of achievement, internalized interest, etc.?)
8. *Place*	(Where does the student work best? Home, school, learning centers, library, media corner?)
9. *Physical Environment and Conditions*	(Floor, carpet, reclining, sitting, desk, temperature, table lighting, type of clothing, food?)
10. *Type of Assignments*	(On which type of assignments does the student thrive? Contracts, totally self-directed projects, teacher-selected tasks, etc.?)

11. *Perceptual Strengths and Styles*   (How does the student learn most easily? Visual materials, sound recording, printed media, tactile experiences, kinesthetic activities, multimedia packages, combinations of these?)

12. *Type of Structure and Evaluation*   (What type of structure suits this student most of the time? Strict, flexible, self-determined, jointly arranged, periodic, self-starting, continuous, occasional, time-line expectations, terminal assessment, etc.?)

One desirable way to begin this individualized inventory is to allow each youngster to analyze his own learning style. Interviews and team analysis can follow as the teacher and other team members become directly involved with the student. The following simple exercise tried under varying conditions will reveal many of the elements previously listed.

Your Learning Style

If a student is not certain as to what is meant by learning style, he can take the following short diagnostic test to determine his personal learning style.

A Diagnostic Test

We would like you to learn and remember a seven-digit telephone number.
Which method of teaching should we use?

1. Tell you the number once or twice and then ask you to *repeat* it
   (a) two minutes later and then, again,
   (b) one day later?
2. Tell you the number once or twice, let you *write* it and then ask you to repeat it
   (a) two minutes later and then, again,
   (b) one day later?
3. Tell you the number once or twice, let you write it, give you a little time to *study* it and then ask you to repeat it
   (a) one hour later and then, again,
   (b) one day later?
4. Tell you the number once or twice, let you write it, give you time to study it and tell you that you will be expected to *dial* it
   (a) one hour later and then, again,
   (b) one day later? (Are you beginning to feel more comfortable?)

5. Give you the number in writing, and indicate that you will be expected to dial the number when you know it, and again one week later?
6. Give you the written number on a slide or film, accompanied by a record that has the spoken number on it, a telephone, a telephone-number game and a pencil and paper—and tell you, "Learn this number any way you want to, but tell us when you think you know it."

Obviously, this last method provides opportunities to capitalize on a student's unique learning style. The technique also reduces pressure and actively engages him in the educational process through the provision of media resource alternatives.[2] Student contracts and the use of alternative procedures and activities are potentially the most powerful teaching tools yet devised to stimulate individualized learning and should be a part of every dynamic educational program.

Individualizing Instruction: The Need and the Task

Individualizing or personalizing instruction simply focuses the emphasis of the instructional process on each individual student—his skills, abilities, interests, learning styles, motivation, goals, rate of learning, self-discipline, problem-solving ability, degree of retention, participation, strengths, weaknesses and prognosis for moving ahead in various curriculum areas and projects. The teacher becomes more professional and assumes the functions of learning facilitator, guide, consultant, professional diagnostician and prescriber of learning resources, activities, evaluation procedures and total learning packages (called contracts) for each student. The process places more responsibility for learning on the student and makes better use of his individual interests, goals and strengths (Photo 1-2).

Once educators recognize that children *are* extremely different from each other in their ability to learn, in their interests and motivation, in their ability to sustain concentration and be self-disciplined and in their perceptual strengths and weaknesses, it will become more evident that most daily class and large-group instruction are inappropriate to long-range, effective learning for the individual.

The *need* for individualizing instruction has been apparent for many years. The process of achieving it, however, is less obvious and

[2]Rita Stafford Dunn and Hamilton S. Blum, *Individualizing Instruction* (New York: Board of Cooperative Educational Services Research and Development Division, 1970), p.10.

Photo 1-2. *Individualization focuses the emphasis of instruction on each student—his skills, interests, learning styles... (Photograph courtesy of Fountain Valley School District, Fountain Valley, California.)*

not fully realized. Schools throughout the nation are beginning to explore ways of changing teaching strategies, organizational patterns and staffing procedures to obtain as much individualization as possible. The change process undoubtedly will differ among schools, districts and sections of the country, depending upon the composition of each student body, teacher and paraprofessional faculty, community population, attitude of each group toward change and the specific need for individualization.

No stress-free, "perfect" guidelines for inducing change can be devised to facilitate the process for all districts. The following necessary steps are offered, however, to foster the development of a positive community environment for change toward individualization.

Before Introducing Individualized Instruction

Diagnosis is the passkey to successful individualization of instruction. Administrators, teachers or committees interested in the adoption of this teaching technique should focus on the following categories in their diagnoses:

A. Present *Teacher* Abilities
   1. Subject matter ability $<$ strengths / weaknesses
   2. Specific *skills* and talents
   3. *Interests* (topics, hobbies, concerns, collections, sports, etc.)
   4. *Leadership* abilities (charisma and focus)
   5. *Organizational* abilities (coordination and cooperation)
   6. *Diagnostic* and prescriptive abilities
   7. Numbers of teachers with
      a. strengths
      b. weaknesses
      c. specific skills and talents
      d. spheres of interest
      e. leadership abilities
      f. organization
      g. diagnostic and prescriptive abilities

B. Present *Pupil* Abilities
   1. Levels of *academic* ability $<$ strengths / weaknesses
   2. Specific *skills* and talents
   3. *Interests* (topics, concerns, hobbies, collections, sports, etc.)
   4. *Self-direction* abilities (motivation)
   5. *Self-discipline* abilities (maturity)
   6. *Perceptual strengths*
   7. *Learning styles*
   8. Numbers of pupils in group with similar
      a. strengths
      b. weaknesses
      c. specific skills and talents
      d. interests
      e. self-direction abilities
      f. self-discipline abilities
      g. perceptual strengths
      h. learning styles

C. Present *Facilities and Resources*

1. Learning spaces open spaces
small-group areas (magic carpets, learning centers, media corners, etc.)
individual areas (carrels, booths, nooks, lounges, study centers)
usable corridors

2. Resource alternatives library
multimedia (machines and films, film loops, listening stations, overhead transparencies, filmstrips, tapes, records, etc.)
art (craft, musical, physical)

3. Professional resources proximity to off-"campus" agencies
access to *personnel* off "campus"
availability of school-related *specialists* (instructional, guidance, psychological, health, sociological)
availability of *extra personnel* (aides, student teachers, parents, community volunteers)

D. Present *Environment*

1. *Administration*

a. Is the "individualizing of instruction" being imposed from "above," or is it an outgrowth of pupil-teacher-administration-community-determined need for improvement?

b. How was this approach selected for introduction into this school (district, building, grade, class)?

c. Were representative administrators, teachers, pupils and community members included in the decision and planning to adopt this program?

d. Is there widespread understanding of individualization? Do administrators, teachers, community representatives and pupils understand its implications for improved education? Do they understand the process of developing and introducing individualization techniques?

e. Has a resonably positive climate for introduction been established?

f. What consideration has been given the training of administrators for leadership roles in introducing and supervising the development of individualization?

g. What consideration has been given the development of an evaluation format (before and after) to determine the merits of the techniques that are used in this school (district, building, class)?

    h. What provisions have been made to modify and improve the program after it begins?

    i. Will use of individualization be voluntary or mandatory?

    j. How widespread will the initial introduction be (pilot program, one grade, primary, one school, districtwide)?

    k. Who will be responsible for organizing the initial project? Who will assist?

    l. How will the program be phased out if it is not successful?

2. *Faculty*

    a. Do the teachers' strengths provide a strong enough base to begin planning for introducing individualized instruction?

    b. What provision is being made for eliminating gaps in teacher strengths?

    c. Can the program be successful in spite of recognized teacher characteristics that require improvement?

    d. What provision is being made to train teachers to use the new techniques effectively? Is the training approach practical?

    e. Will teachers be permitted released time or extra compensation for the training?

    f. Has the teachers' representative organization been involved in discussions and planning for the new program?

    g. Is there reasonable certainty that the teachers will be willing to try the new techniques?

    h. Will adequate help and guidance be provided in the school to facilitate the teachers' efforts?

    i. Will the teachers be included in the evaluation of the program?

3. *Community*

    a. Have community representatives been involved in discussions and planning for the individualization of instruction?

    b. Is there reasonable certainty that the community will support the school's efforts toward changing the instructional system?

    c. Will parents be apprised of how, when and to what extent the changes will take place? Will they be permitted to observe the process at times? Will they be invited to help?

    d. Has adequate news coverage been afforded to the contemplated change? Has the community response been essentially positive?

    e. Who will be responsible for keeping the community informed of progress and appraisals?

    f. Are community attitude surveys (before, during and after) advisable?

4. *Pupils*

    a. Have pupil representatives been involved in discussions and planning for the individualization of instruction? Have their ideas and suggestions been seriously considered?

b. What provisions will be made to help pupils adjust to the new programs? Will extra training and guidance be available to those pupils who find it difficult to adapt themselves to a changed instructional method?

c. How will pupils be apprised of how well they are achieving in the new system? Will remedial or enrichment help be available to the exceptional student who requires training not available through use of present faculty skills?

Once these assessments have been made (objectively), determinations of *how* to proceed should follow.

If a technique or program of instruction is to be implemented successfully, every key person involved in the educational system must be committed to its value and play an important role in its initiation.

How to Organize for Individualized Instruction

A.   *What Administration Must Do*

1. Tabulate, appraise and categorize results of the teacher, pupil and faculty diagnoses.
2. Identify leadership ("key") administrators, teachers, pupils and community representatives.
3. Purchase additional appropriate media and curricula resources, based upon teacher and pupil identification, the number of qualified teachers available to instruct and the estimated number of pupils to participate.
4. Identify resource personnel to fill the gaps in areas lacking teacher strength.
5. Provide clerical aid and student-teacher personnel assistance for the teachers. [It is a good idea to invite the local teacher education colleges to assign junior and senior trainees to your school so that they may be included in the preadoption and planning discussions and then be trained (with staff) to participate in the program as assistants in the classrooms.]
6. Serve as constant liaison among teachers, community representatives, pupils, resource personnel, clerks, aides, student teachers, beginning teachers, etc.

B.   *What Teachers Must Do*

1. Determine one or more curriculum areas appropriate to your own knowledge, skills and talents, or those for which you would not mind learning new skills or additional information.
2. Identify every possible kind of instructional material appropriate to the selected curriculum area or the particular aspect of it that you will coordinate (every level of reading material, music, poetry, dance, films, records, loops, tapes, etc.). Familiarize yourself with these and categorize them for easy accessibility.

3. Identify the academic levels and skills of the pupils you will be teaching.

4. Determine a tentative beginning introduction for large-group instruction. Clarify the most pertinent concepts, your reasons for being interested in individualization and the ground rules you would like followed by the pupils.

5. Coordinate your aspect of the curriculum with the other teachers involved in this program. Determine which areas you will introduce, reinforce, enrich, coordinate, team-teach, etc.

6. Advise administration of any weaknesses you see inherent in the program. Try to eliminate potential failure cooperatively before the program is begun. Continue this process during the program.

7. Invite the parents of your pupils to a meeting where you can explain the overriding philosophy of individualizing instruction. Encourage questioning and answer as honestly and as positively as you can. You need not have "all the answers"; parents will wecome your sincerity if you admit that this is a new program that has excellent potential but that everyone concerned with it will have to carefully scrutinize and evaluate it as it progresses. If you are committed to trying because of the projected improvements it can offer, the parents will be equally as objective or positive.

8. Arrange for an individual meeting with each child admitted into your phase of the program. Get to know him or her. Encourage open discussion. Discover the individual facets, interests, abilities and learning styles of each child. This information will become apparent as you get to know the child better and diagnose his needs with other teachers and aides.

9. Map out a beginning instructional program for a few (1-5) children, based on the information submitted by the administration, former teachers, anecdotal records, test scores, indicated skills and talents. Keep the assignments or contracts on the child's level of academic operation. Build in the next step of more complicated learning. Identify children with similar skills and talents who might form task forces or groups with each other. Be certain that you have enough materials available on each academic level for each pupil.

10. Develop a recording system for each child. Begin a file which includes the results of the child's diagnostic tests and interviews, his contracts and any information you consider pertinent. When the child's Self-Test has been successfully completed, add that to the file. Also add the child's Terminal Test, whether or not he scores to the degree of proficiency required. Grades should be determined on the basis of the *quality* of completed work in relation to the pupil's perceived ability. Assignments and grades should be carefully discussed with the pupil so that he understands what to do, how to do it and how to indicate his perceptions and understanding of what he has learned.

11. At the beginning of the program, teach every child assigned to you how to work quietly or with activity level sound which does not disturb others, obtain help when needed, use available media equipment, work in pairs and groups, assist other youngsters, accept criticism, offer criticism, report learnings, present findings, etc. These are the skills necessary to the successful functioning of an individualized instructional program.

12. Order all the supplies you will need to conduct an effective program.

13. Recognize that every aspect of the entire program need not be individually prescribed. A stimulating program is one that incorporates some large- and a great deal of small-group instruction in conjunction with an essentially individualized approach in terms of the pupil's ability, skills, interests, learning styles and rate of growth. The combination of these instructional patterns produces a varied, effective learning environment.

C. *What Parents Who Wish to Participate May Do*

1. Read good professional articles and books that explain and describe the individualization of instruction.

2. Realize that what was done somewhere else may have been appropriate to that institution (district, building, etc.) but that varying conditions, faculties and students demand different or modified approaches.

3. Voice your apprehensions (if any) and try to be objective about the explanations offered.

4. Offer suggestions for possible improvement if you perceive areas where change may be preferable; do not be offended if your suggestions are not accepted. They may be held in abeyance until "the time is right."

5. Volunteer assistance if you are able to contribute on a continuing basis. Do not be offended if your offer is not accepted. If it is, do not usurp the teacher's authority. Do not believe that you can replace the teacher or that the children relate better to you. Understand that your responsibility is to assist the teacher to help the children. Do not be critical of the teacher, the administration or the system. Be supportive and pleasant. If you are at all suspicious of the effectiveness of the new technique, voice your qualms in a neatly recorded report and submit it to the teacher. You may wish to send a carbon copy to the administration after the teacher has had the opportunity to react. Do not discuss your thoughts or the results of your conference with your child's teacher, other teachers or parents. Always behave ethically and try to observe the protocol of the school. Professional behavior requires that administrators and teachers most closely involved are apprised of conditions first—and in confidence.

6. Accept your assignment to visit (assist) as a *learning* experience for you.

Frequency, Intensity and Variety:
The Three Keys to Effective Teaching and Learning

Students can absorb any information to which they are exposed, providing they are brought into contact with the items frequently, in a variety of ways and with intensity. An easy equation for this rule is:

"FIVE": *F*requency, *In*tensity and *V*ariety = *Eff*ective teaching and learning.

"Frequency" does not suggest that a child should write each spelling word half a dozen times to ensure retention; indeed, straight "drill" may be a poor teaching technique, unless the child has revealed through diagnostic testing that he can learn only through repetitious writing (a rare idiosyncrasy). Rather, appropriate frequency is best woven into an interdisciplinary approach wherein selected concepts and facts are presented many times through their use in different curriculum areas or spheres of interest, so that the child is repeatedly exposed to the same information in many interesting ways and in different contexts.

In addition to the use of repetition in an interdisciplinary approach, frequency implies that after initial presentation, a multitude of learning resources, activities, projects, small-group interactions and pupil-teacher conferences will reiterate the material that should be learned.

"Variety" suggests that a multimedia approach to learning be used by students and teachers to permit students to hear, see, touch and be personally involved with concepts and facts through books, pictures, films, slides, filmstrips, records, tapes, transparencies, loops, television, TV cassettes and other learning resources that may be available. Repeated exposure (frequency) to selected studies through multiple learning resources (variety) tends to reinforce the material in the student's memory and within a conscious frame of reference.

"Intensity" is provided by the exposure to material through media that complement the individual's perceptual strengths (learning style). Intensity is also generated by the focus and stress placed on specific studies by the teacher, the contract, the student himself (his interests and concerns) or his peers. In some cases, the requirements that must be fulfilled (as established by the teacher or the contract) place sufficient demand upon the student to cause him to

VERNON REGIONAL
JUNIOR COLLEGE LIBRARY

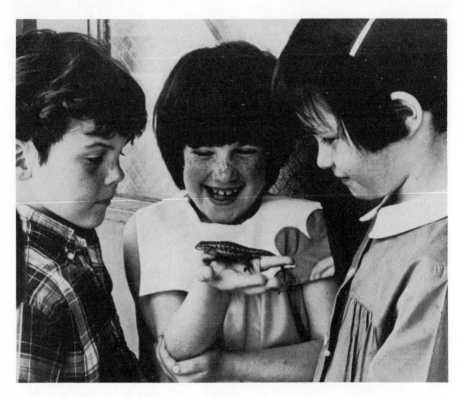

Photo 1-3 *Visual-tactile learning provides intensity and variety. (Bell & Howell, Audio-Visual Products Division, Chicago, Illinois.)*

feel a direct emotional interaction with the material. Self-motivation through interest is a key factor in providing intensity.

Students who are exposed to information frequently, intensely and with variety, will embrace learning and tend to retain what they have absorbed (Photo 1-3).

How to Vary Instruction According to Needs: Contracts, Team Learning and Other Teaching Strategies

An effective instructional program recognizes and provides for the different learning styles of individuals by:

1. Diagnosing each student's perceptual strengths and weaknesses and then providing learning methods and materials that capitalize on the revealed strengths.

2. Diagnosing each student's academic ability in each curriculum area and then:
   (a) prescribing a program that will build on the revealed academic strengths and reduce the revealed academic weaknesses;
   (b) providing learning materials on the level of academic comprehension revealed through the diagnosis;
   (c) providing a variety of learning materials to stimulate curiosity, offer repetition without reducing interest and create a personal involvement with the act of learning for the student.
3. Recognizing each student's special interests, hobbies, skills, talents or motivations and incorporating these, wherever appropriate, into the child's curriculum.

Once the teacher has correctly diagnosed the student, she must then design a flexible program of study that the student will be expected to master. This program is called a *prescription* and includes a listing of the instructional objectives (curriculum requirements, course of study or educational goals) specifically written for the individual student in behavioral terms.

The student bears the responsibility for learning what is included in his prescription. The teacher serves as a facilitator and guide in the learning process. The role of the teacher includes acting as diagnostician, prescriber and guide. The role of the student is that of self-teacher.

In contrast to the informality of the British primary schools where most of the curriculum is unstructured (designed, but waiting to be discovered as the child develops interest and perception), an effective instructional system must incorporate a variety of specifically designed teaching and learning strategies so that learning occurs by plan, not just by accident. Just as students should not be required to learn through only one or two resources, they should not be required to learn through only one method. Any one method may not be suitable for a specific individual, and, furthermore, the utilization of many methods permits the teacher to expose students to the same curriculum with frequency, variety and intensity.

Contracts

A contract is a prescription (topic, course of study, unit) written for, by or with the student. It provides many opportunities for a youngster to learn independently, and, ideally, includes a variety of learning resources (tapes, records, books, films, pictures, loops, slides, games, etc.) through which he may gather the required information.

Contracts should include, in addition to clear statements of the prescription (the behavioral objectives), a listing of many kinds of learning resources and a series of activity alternatives whereby the student has a choice in determining how he will apply the information he has collected. The contract also includes a series of reporting alternatives, so that the information that has been gathered and applied will be shared with individuals and small groups.

When a diagnostic test, a student self-assessment test and a terminal test are added, the contract becomes a Contract Activity Package (CAP).

Contracts enable each student to work independently at the rate that is comfortable for him. It eliminates the need for a youngster to "keep up" with and achieve to the same depth as every other student and permits individual pacing, growth, selection of materials and focusing in relation to interest. Contracts also provide time for the teacher to work closely with individuals as needed. For a detailed description of contracts and contract activity packages, turn to Chapters 3 and 4.

Team Learning

Team learning is an excellent instructional technique through which students form small groups (five to eight) that cooperatively try to teach themselves required facts and concepts which are common to each team member's prescription (contract, assignment, unit or topic).

The team is given concrete (written or recorded) materials which include the body of information that must be mastered. The members may read the material individually or collectively, however they decide. A set of questions that the team must answer follows the written or recorded selection. Some of the questions are directly answerable in terms of the presented information; some of the questions have no definite answers and require group interaction, discussion and decision making. One member serves as the team recorder and notes the answers that the group develops collectively.

Team learning is an excellent way of introducing new material and ideas to students and it prevents the alienation that may occur when students work independently and alone all the time. It is an extremely effective teaching strategy because it utilizes team or group learning and focuses attention upon the material in several different ways, requiring the students to think about the specific and related materials, discuss them, reach decisions and then report to a larger group or the teacher. In more sophisticated versions, team learning provides frequency, variety and intensity of the given prescription at least four times during one lesson. For additional details and descriptions read Chapter 5.

Circles of Knowledge

Just as team learning is effective as a method for introducing new material, circles of knowledge (or learning circles) act as its counterpart, providing an enticing way of reviewing material that has already been learned.

Students are grouped in terms of the similarity of their prescriptions and whether or not they have completed a selected aspect of their contract, assignment, unit or topic. The participants may have completed the selected aspect months, weeks, days or merely hours before each other, but, if they have covered that topic, they may participate in the circle of knowledge. For directions on how to form the groupings, present the task and utilize the technique to greatest advantage, turn to Chapter 5.

Simulations

Educational simulations have been produced in industry and education by adults, but bright and skillful students may also write simulations that are appropriate to the individual classroom situation.

Simulations present hypothetical situations that are based upon something that may very well occur within the lives of the participants. Students are required to either "play a role" or portray how they would actually behave in the projected situation—the object being: (a) the development of alternative solutions to a given problem and (b) the development of and experience with problem-solving skills.

Simulations can become very real to those who work within them[3] and frequently provide the "players" with insights and understandings that they previously had not achieved. Chapter 6 includes extensive information about this method and differentiates between it and another interesting technique, role playing.

Role Playing

Whereas a simulation usually focuses on seeking solutions to given problems, role playing enables students to demonstrate their

---

[3] Carter, Dunn, Dunn, Kleinmann and Stealey, *A Report: Second Annual Conference* (New York: The Education Council, 1968), p. 14.

reactions or perceptions to situations and persons without the necessity of utilizing cognitive skills that may be as yet undeveloped in some youngsters. Role playing is a simple technique which is essentially used as a review or orientation process; simulations build on experience and require extensions of absorbed information into critical thinking abilities.

Case Studies

Case studies can be used by individuals or small groups to develop critical thinking skills and gain new perception into concepts and issues. The technique may be used in a simple way with young children who have fairly long attention spans or it may constitute an entire unit for advanced students who wish to focus intensely on a given area. Chapter 7 provides practical guidelines and samples for use in different areas of the educational system.

Brainstorming

Brainstorming may be conducted in either simple or more sophisticated ways, depending upon the skill of the teacher and the intelligence and background of the students.

In its elementary form, it requires interactions based on some background information already possessed by the students, who then serve as catalysts for each other's ideas. In its complex stage, participants are led (or lead themselves) through a process of goal setting or objectives development, analysis, evaluation, creative problem solving and reanalysis for action. This topic is covered more thoroughly in Chapter 7.

Other Instructional Techniques

Teachers construct motivating and stimulating instructional environments for students when they provide multiple opportunities for both independent and small-group learning. Many youngsters enjoy working alone, but require interaction with others to synthesize their thinking and elicit reactions to their conclusions or perceptions. Other youngsters prefer learning with their peers, claiming that it sharply reduces their anxiety and fear of failure. These children should be given periodic opportunities to work independently in addition to the experiences designed for group learning. Most youngsters enjoy and profit from a variety of learning experiences. Thus the adoption of many teaching techniques induces students to remain interested and absorbed in what they are learning.

The final chapter in this book discusses spheres of interest and explains how task forces, tutoring teams, committees, community and work-centered experiences, the open campus and the use of multimedia projects can further involve students in becoming responsible and self-directive learners.

The following chart (Figure 1-1) illustrates 13 different instructional techniques and suggests appropriate group numbers, age levels and curriculum areas for effective utilization.

The Differences Between Programed Learning Sequences and Individualized Instruction

Programed learning was one of the first steps toward individualizing instruction and very successfully provided opportunities for students to move ahead at a pace that was appropriate for their own learning abilities.

Students were prediagnosed and then programed into a sequence at the point of entry that most closely coincided with their revealed level of academic ability. From there on, every student either sequentially progressed through or skipped over identical materials and content in exactly the same way. The only factor that actually was individualized was the *rate of speed* with which he completed the sequence. This approach might be defined as "individualized pacing."

Instruction that is truly individualized must be designed by the teacher who knows the student and has tested and diagnosed his various abilities. The teacher is then able to prescribe a program tailored to the youngster's abilities, weaknesses, learning style, interests and degree of self-discipline. Such a prescription not only permits the student to proceed at his own pace and level, but on materials and projects that motivate and involve him. The student is provided with alternative resources and encouraged to exercise much choice in the selection of activities, reporting, self-assessment, self-instruction and methodology.

A prescription cannot be prepackaged or preprogramed and still be individualized in any way other than to permit self-pacing. Industrial and educational groups have developed praiseworthy sequences that they label "individualized" and then simultaneously prescribe for every child in the country who scores approximately at the same academic or age level.

INSTRUCTIONAL TECHNIQUES

SUGGESTED FOR EFFECTIVE UTILIZATION

● Most Effective
○ Somewhat Effective

INSTRUCTIONAL TECHNIQUES	No. in Group	Age Levels	CURRICULUM AREAS				
			Language	Math	Science	Social Studies	Problem Solving
Team Learning	5-8	5-18	●	●	●	●	●
Simulations	5-8	9-18	●	○	○	●	●
Role Playing	1-9	5-18	●	●	●	●	●
Learning Activity Packages	1-6	5-18	●	●	●	●	○
Independent Contracts	1	5-18	●	●	●	●	○
Team Task Force	3-6	5-18	●	●	●	●	●
Tutoring Teams	1-5	5-18	●	●	●	●	○
Circles of Knowledge	5-10	8-18	●	○	○	●	○
Brainstorming	5-30	5-18	●	○	●	○	●
Multimedia Projects	1-30	5-18	●	●	●	●	●
Community Contributions	1-30	12-18	●	●	●	●	●
Working While Learning	1-30	14-18	●	●	●	●	●
Case Studies	1-30	9-18	●	○	○	●	●

Figure 1-1

Content of Individualized Prescriptions

A prescription is not individualized unless the subject matter within a given curriculum focuses on concepts and data that are relevant and interesting to the student. It is fallacious to assume that a well-written story will be absorbing to every child in a class or school. Interest is determined by inner motivation, not necessarily by exposure to materials that are judged very good by adults or some students. An individualized program permits youngsters to learn in depth about those things that they find intriguing or meaningful.

Learning sequences that provide the same content for every child on a given academic or age level do not individualize instructional content.

Resources for Individualized Prescriptions

A prescription is not individualized unless it provides learning materials on varied academic levels through many different learning resources, so that the youngster who learns well by listening can learn through tapes, records, lectures, sound tracks and other auditory mechanisms, while the youngster who learns easily by viewing may learn through the use of books, pictures, films, slides, video tapes or other visual means. Similarly, children who require tactile and kinesthetic experiences must have those resources built into their prescription.

Learning sequences that rely heavily on printed matter alone have not individualized the instructional resources.

Activities for Individualized Prescriptions

Most programed sequences require the completion of specific assignments or activities before the student can continue into the next sequence. A prescription is not individualized unless the learner is permitted considerable *choice* in the selection of both activities and assignments.

Learning sequences that require completion of the same activities for each youngster on a given academic level do not individualize the processes through which acquired information can be used or applied.

Methods for Individualized Prescriptions

A prescription is not individualized unless students are permitted and encouraged to experience a variety of instructional techniques to determine the ways in which they respond most easily to the learning process. Students should be channeled into independent study, team learning, circles of knowledge, brainstorming, simulations, task forces, case studies and other procedures for acquiring knowledge.

Learning sequences that rely heavily on only one or two methods of instruction (usually listening and question-and-answer discussion) cannot claim to be individualizing through the use of appropriate teaching strategies.

Student Involvement for Individualized Prescriptions

A prescription that is prepackaged usually has been written for an "average" student who has scored a particular achievement index or grade in a selected curriculum area. This packaged material does not take into account the personal differences that are found among all children. There is no opportunity for revision of wording or content, unless each individual teacher elects to incorporate additions or deletions in the sequence based upon her perception of the materials in relation to the student. Once the teacher is required to alter the materials to provide the flexibility that is required for individualization, she is revising the programed materials. Revision is probably as time-consuming as development, and is certainly not as effective.

In an individualized program, where the teacher actually designs a learning package for the student, the student may be directly involved in the development of the materials, resources, activities and methods through which he will learn. His interests, motivations, skills, talents and personal experiences may serve as a framework within which the program can be designed. It is also desirable to permit students to write their own sequences, once they have demonstrated their abilities to recognize content value and appropriate learning resources and methods.

A prescription that does not directly involve the student in its creation may be partially individualized (paced) but will probably be less attractive and motivating to the student.

Organization of Program for Individualized Prescriptions

The programed learning sequences that have been widely introduced into our schools to date are school-based packages that are intended to either replace or supplement the teacher's efforts to teach children while they are in the classroom.

The concept that learning occurs either only or essentially in a school building is recognized as fallacious by most professionals. Experimentation with "open campus" programs where students attend classes as they need or desire, has revealed that much of the time youngsters spend in educational establishments could be reduced into more fruitful and meaningful experiences. The Parkway High School in Philadelphia, Pennsylvania, where students are permitted to utilize industry and the entire urban community as a learning laboratory, served to attract and retain youngsters who were considered to be potential and actual dropouts, by creating a meaningful and dynamic educational environment. The Murray Road School, Newton, Massachusetts, placed the development of courses and choice of faculty entirely in the hands of the students and faculty.

An individualized program must consider how much *time* the student is capable of spending in study and concentration during a given day. It must also evaluate the *time of day or night* during which the individual appears to be most productive or able to focus and achieve. It must appraise the environment in which the student can best relax and learn. Some people can learn only when "curled up" on a comfortable couch or bed (a large, soft expanse), while others require the discipline of stiff, hard-backed chairs, a table and a clock. Students have revealed that differences in learning environments include temperature variations, the need for food or liquid intake, silence or sound (often music), lighting, lengthy periods of concentration or shorter ones, more frequent periods of learning, aloneness or group interaction, "breaks" or concentrated focus, the use of one or two resources or many media materials (tapes, films, slides, records, television), single or multiple equipment and "deadlines" or self-pacing over a prescribed period of time. The variety of approaches may vary from student to student or for the same youngster at different times.

Considering the many factors needed to design a student's prescription, programed learning sequences that require the student's presence in the classroom or at a desk at home do not really individualize. Instead, packages should be prescribed that permit the student flexibility in determining *where* he will learn, *when* he will learn, *how* he will learn and with *whom*. Classrooms and the teacher should serve as available resources but should not be mandated.

Youngsters who are able to achieve their prescribed objectives, and who demonstrate their ability to be self-motivated and self-disciplined, should not be restricted to limited patterns that are prescribed by others. Rather, these students should be given the responsibility for mastering their prescriptions as they deem best, even when they determine that they are able to complete entire assignments or contracts through the use of resources at home (or in other acceptable locations). Such students might not appear in "school" for many of their self-directed experiences. Conferences with the teacher on the initial diagnosis, the development of the prescription or program, the selection of resources, conferences and activities with peers and other resource persons and the terminal assessment (testing) to determine the extent and proficiency of their learning are some of the activities that may require a student's appearance at school or organized learning centers.

Arguments will be advanced that this procedure will not prove effective with all children, and the authors agree. However, for those students for whom it proves to be effective, this approach should be available as an option.

Once students demonstrate that they are proficient at determining when, where, how and with whom they elect to study and master their instructional objectives, they should be given the *choice* of whether they are to continue in a given pattern or select another (perhaps totally different) mode of learning. The self-motivated, self-disciplined student should be *trusted* and *expected* to complete individually prescribed prescriptions successfully.

When students demonstrate that they are not able to discipline themselves to study and master their prescriptions, the freedom of choosing the time, place and mode in which they will learn may be withdrawn. However, teachers who have used independent and curriculum contract activity packages have reported that many youngsters who were previously undisciplined and unmotivated, *became* conscientious and dependable learners when teacher expectations were raised and they were permitted increased independence and responsibility.

The differences between programed learning sequences, which are designed for mass use, and an authentically individualized program, include the potential for greater motivation, self-direction and achievement.

Understanding Organizational Patterns

A school's organizational pattern is determined by the way its pupils and teachers are assigned to each other for instructional purposes.

Ideally, instruction occurs through a variety of "methods" (teaching and learning strategies and techniques) and is not directly related to the organizational pattern. In practice, however, the organizational pattern determines the allocation of resources, the accessibility of media and personnel and, to some extent, the selection of curriculum matter.

Individualization, which is a basic instructional approach, may be used successfully in every organizational pattern but is more easily introduced when differentiated staff patterns (teachers, assistants, paraprofessionals, student-teachers, parents, older students, resource persons, etc.) and extensive media are available.

Once a school has individualized its program for students, its organizational pattern tends to gradually diffuse into multiple variations of several patterns that the school's professional personnel recognize as most appropriate and effective for use in their particular situation. As programs continue to respond to the revealed needs and abilities of staff and students, the organizational structure becomes more flexible and tends to adopt aspects of team teaching (cooperative responsibility for the instruction of students among teachers), "no bell" (student selection of curriculum area emphasis), sphere of interest (direct student involvement in the determination of curriculum), nongradedness (student advancement at a rate consistent with abilities) and some departmentalization (major responsibility for student academic growth, placed with professional teachers who demonstrate expertise in a given curriculum area).

The following grid (Figure 1-2) outlines the characteristics of several major organizational patterns and differentiated-staffing patterns when employed in a school system. Open campus,[4] which basically is a highly flexible process, is still in its experimental stages but facilitates the introduction of individualization to the extent where traditional organizational patterns may be completely eliminated within the next 10 years.

---

[4] In a unanimous decision, the Massachusetts State Board of Education approved a recommendation by State Education Commissioner Neil V. Sullivan, permitting them to operate "open high school programs in which all students need not be present at all times." The statewide program, which officials claim is unique in the nation, permits students to be scheduled in programs of less than 5.5 hours of formal instruction or in programs where student learning is partially self-directed within or outside a high school. Participating schools are still required to provide the regular 5.5-hour program for those who want it. The decision was based on the success of three pilot programs in Brookline, Winchester and Falmouth as reported in *Education, U.S.A.,* Fall, 1970, p. 80.

Figure 1-2: Organizational Patterns

CHARACTERISTICS	SELF-CONTAINED CLASSROOM	TEAM TEACHING	MULTI-, UN-, NONGRADED	NO BELL
TEACHER APPRAISAL	Individual teacher perspective of student ability and growth in all curriculum areas.*	Cooperative-teacher perspectives of student ability and growth in selected curriculum areas.†	Depends upon whether group is nongraded in a self-contained or teamed situation.‡	Cooperative teacher perspectives of student ability and growth in student-selected curriculum areas.§
PEER RELATIONSHIPS	Permits development of strong peer group ties.	Permits development of strong peer group ties.	Permits development of strong peer group ties.	Permits development of strong peer interest ties.#
TEACHER RESPONSIBILITY	Requires the teacher to teach in multiple curriculum areas.	Permits the teacher to teach in area(s) of curriculum expertise.	Depends upon whether group is nongraded in a self-contained or teamed situation.	Permits teaching in area(s) of curriculum expertise.
INSTRUCTIONAL TECHNIQUES	Demands individual knowledge and supervision of large- and small- group instructional techniques.	Permits cooperative knowledge of and assignments in large- and small- group instructional techniques.	Depends upon whether group is nongraded in a self-contained or teamed situation.	Permits cooperative knowledge and use of large- and small- group instructional techniques.
STUDENT INTEREST				Provides increased opportunities for students to concentrate on interests.
STUDENT GROWTH	Unless individualized, tends to move students ahead as a class or in groups.	Unless individualized, tends to move students ahead as a class or in groups.	Theoretically moves students ahead at "their own pace"; in practice, unless individualized, tends to move students ahead in groups.	Unless individualized, tends to move students ahead as a class or in groups.
MEDIA AND MATERIALS	If individualized, requires extensive media and materials in every curriculum area.	If individualized, requires extensive media and materials in areas of curriculum expertise.	Depends upon whether group is nongraded in a self-contained or in a teamed situation.	Requires extensive media and materials in area(s) of curriculum expertise.
TEACHER PLANNING	Permits individual teacher planning.	Requires team planning.	Depends upon whether group is nongraded in a self-contained or teamed situation.	Permits individual teacher planning.
TEACHER EFFECTIVENESS††	Maximum teacher effectiveness usually occurs with homogeneous pupil grouping.	Maximum teacher effectiveness occurs with homogeneous pupil grouping.	Maximum teacher effectiveness occurs with homogeneous pupil grouping.	Maximum teacher effectiveness occurs with homogeneous pupil grouping.

*See page 54 for footnotes to Figure 1-2.

MODULAR SCHEDULING	*SPHERE OF INTEREST*	*BRITISH PRIMARY*	*DEPARTMENTAL*	
Individual teacher perspectives of student ability and growth combined into overall profile.	Cooperative teacher perspectives of student ability and growth in all curriculum areas.	Either individual or cooperative teacher perspective of student ability and growth in all curriculum areas.	Individual teacher perspectives of student ability and growth in each curriculum area, combined into overall profile.	Cooperative staff perspective of student ability and growth in all curriculum areas.
Permits development of peer group ties.**	Permits development of strong peer interest ties.	Permits development of strong peer group ties.	Permits development of peer group ties.	Permits development of strong peer group ties if student group remains together for most of their instruction.
Permits teaching in area(s) of curriculum expertise.	Permits teaching in area(s) of curriculum expertise.	Depends on whether the group is self-contained or cooperatively taught.	Permits teaching in area(s) of curriculum expertise.	Permits teaching in area of curriculum expertise and provides additional personnel for assistance.
Permits cooperative knowledge and use of large- and small- group instructional techniques.	Permits cooperative knowledge and use of large- and small- group instructional techniques.	Depends on whether the group is self-contained or cooperatively taught.	Demands individual knowledge and supervision of large- and small-group instructional techniques.	Permits cooperative knowledge and use of large- and small- group instructional techniques.
	Provides increased opportunities for students to concentrate on interests and long-range goals.	Provides increased opportunities for students to concentrate on interests.		Provides additional personnel to respond to student interests.
Unless individualized, tends to move students ahead as a class or in groups.	Unless individualized, tends to move students ahead as a class or in groups.	Less tendency to move students ahead as a class and more toward moving them ahead as a group; provides much opportunity for individual growth, but restricts the amount of time the teacher has for each child.	Unless individualized, tends to move students ahead as a class or in groups.	Unless in individualized system, tends to move students ahead as a group; provides more adults for individual student attention.
Requires extensive media and materials in area(s) of curriculum expertise.	Requires extensive media and materials in area(s) of curriculum expertise.	Requires extensive media and materials in every curriculum area.	Requires extensive media and materials in area(s) of curriculum expertise.	Requires extensive media and materials in area(s) of curriculum expertise.
Permits individual teacher planning.	Requires group teacher planning.	Depends on whether the group is self-contained or cooperatively taught.	Permits individual teacher planning.	Requires staff planning.
Maximum teacher effectiveness occurs with homogeneous pupil grouping.	Maximum teacher effectiveness occurs with homogeneous pupil grouping, but responds favorably to a tolerable amount of heterogeneity.	Maximum teacher effectiveness occurs with homogeneous pupil grouping, but responds favorably to heterogeneity.	Maximum teacher effectiveness occurs with homogeneous pupil grouping.	Maximum teacher effectiveness occurs with homogeneous grouping, but responds favorably to a tolerable amount of heterogeneity.

Footnotes for Figure 1-2

*When the teacher is a skilled, sensitive diagnostician, an individual teacher's analysis may permit evaluation of "the whole" child. When the teacher is not an extremely able diagnostician, pupil analysis by one instructor is a distinct disadvantage to most students.

+When each of the teamed (or cooperating) teachers is a skilled and/or sensitive diagnostician, shared professional analysis is preferable to one instructor's appraisal. The value of the diagnosis increases in direct proportion to the ability of the diagnostician(s) as individuals and as a cooperating team.

‡Nongradedness may occur in both self-contained and team-teaching organizational patterns, although less likely in the former.

§A unique feature of the "no bell" system is that it permits students to select curriculum areas on which they wish to concentrate for a given period during the day (afternoons). For the remainder of the school day they are required to complete studies in each of the curriculum areas, with more focus (and time) permitted in the area of highest motivation (interest).

‖Differentiated staffing is not an organizational pattern, but, rather, emphasizes staff deployment in any organizational pattern. "Staff" need not necessarily be limited to professionally certified teachers and may include paraprofessional and clerical assistants, student teachers, parents, community resource personnel and older students assigned to a team on a continuing basis.

#Both the "no bell" and sphere-of-interest patterns permit extensive student involvement in the determination of curriculum concentrations. Student interest, therefore, is enhanced through the provision of many opportunities for development and/or expansion.

**Weaker peer-group ties develop among students who meet for only one subject area than for those who spend most of a school day together. Similarity-of-interest ties, however, tend to develop comparatively stronger bonds among students.

++The comparisons are made because of the realities of grouping; individualization would remove the need to consider outmoded assumptions about homogeneous and heterogeneous grouping.

2

Individualizing Instruction: How to Begin a Program in Your School or Classroom

Involving Teachers in a New Process

Innovation should not be attempted without full, uncompromised support for the training of all personnel who will be directly and actively involved in its implementation. Administrators, teachers, clerical assistants, paraprofessionals, resource persons, parents and students should work together in designing and initiating an innovation such as an individualized instructional program. All those concerned must be exposed jointly to the same concepts and strategies. Although the methods used and the amount of time for each group may vary, the philosophy and goals of individualization must be understood, and strong consensus for implementation must exist if it (or any innovation) is to succeed.

In addition to the *inclusion* of all personnel directly involved, it is strongly urged that the *techniques of individualization be used as the training vehicle.* In this way all participants will have experienced the procedures themselves, and they will be better able to transfer their new approaches to the classroom. This method also allows each professional to appraise, adapt and modify various procedures to his own abilities, personality and interests.

Another value of using the actual techniques of individualization in the in-service institute is the likelihood that teachers will adopt many new instructional techniques that will be effective in their classrooms—even if they eventually decide that the total individualization approach is not for them. If the design of such a training program includes a variety of stimulating teaching strategies, many will undoubtedly find their way into the instructional process.

It is important that teachers do not attempt to individualize every curriculum area within a single term or year. The development of contracts and the accumulation of resources and materials should be phased over an extended period of time. Contracts, for example, may be introduced for a portion of each class in selected subject areas. A developmental approach will prevent the "overwhelmed" syndrome and allow for modifications and improvements as the innovation is implemented.

Publicity Releases

An attractive, well-designed brochure will have the advantage of gaining attention. The information should be presented concisely, with a strong focus on providing aid for the teacher.

Devise a title for the intended program that will clearly explain its purpose. Design "how to" training sessions, workshops and institutes.

State the name of the person(s) who will be responsible for conducting the workshop(s), where and when the program will be held and the exact number of hours required for attendance.

A short description of the program should be placed at the beginning. Examples of appropriate descriptions would include:

- This institute will be designed to meet your personal needs in learning and putting new techniques into practice in your classroom. At last, someone who has done it successfully will demonstrate *how* you can prescribe individual programs for your students without working 20 hours a day to develop the materials.
- Join a seminar that is guaranteed to wake you up from 3:30 to 5:30. This program will not only gain credits for you on the salary schedule, it will aid in making teaching and learning more exciting and pleasurable for both you and your students. Have you tried team learning? Brainstorming? Simulations? Can you construct a contract that allows a student to work by himself or with others independent of further direction from you? Do you now have the time to counsel each student? Join us in the library and in *your* classroom *to learn how.*

Providing potential registrants with short biographical sketches of the instructor may entice them into joining the workshop. The descriptive background material serves to initiate a relationship between the learner and the instructor. Be certain that the instructor has had practical experience working with children, for nothing alienates teachers as much as university professors or "experts" who theorize on a scholarly level and are incapable of actually demonstrating what they have recommended.

In one or two sentences, indicate the required qualifications of those who wish to apply. These questions will aid in establishing the criteria for admission: Will the workshop be designed for early childhood, primary, intermediate, junior high or high school teachers? Is team registration necessary or will individual members of a school (grade, district, discipline) be accepted? Will the series be restricted to specific curriculum areas; e.g., social studies and language arts or mathematics and science? Will in-service credit be granted, and how much?

When specific procedures must be followed, include the information in the brochure. For example:

● Participants desiring in-service credit for this workshop should obtain prior approval from their school's district superintendent. This workshop will involve 15 2-hour sessions, or 30 hours of participation. Required and recommended reading lists will be distributed during the sessions, and each participant will complete one project that he will use with his own students.

Workshop Outlines

Providing the participants with an overview of what will be included in the series will prepare them for active participation and apprise them of what they may expect. Each instructor should design an institute that best conforms to his/her own teaching style, but the following are some of the items that must be included in a workshop devoted to developing teaching strategies appropriate to individualization of instruction:

1. Understanding the differences among children's:
   (a) perceptual strengths and weaknesses,
   (b) intelligence levels,
   (c) achievement levels,
   (d) motivation,
   (e) self-discipline,
   (f) interests,
   (g) attention spans,
   (h) learning styles.
2. The methods of individualization that permit a youngster to learn:
   (a) at his own pace,

  (b) on his own level,
  (c) for periods of time appropriate to his ability to sustain attention, discipline and motivation,
  (d) through his major interests,
  (e) through alternative media resources and methods.
3. Effective instructional techniques; e.g.:
  (a) contracts and contract activity packages,
  (b) team learning,
  (c) circles of knowledge,
  (d) brainstorming,
  (e) case studies,
  (f) simulations,
  (g) role playing,
  (h) task forces,
  (i) group analysis.
4. The role of media and technology in individualization.
5. Classroom organizational and school staffing patterns.
6. Diagnostic skills and techniques.
7. Supervised implementation of theories, concepts, methods and use of equipment in the classrooms of the participants.

Teachers should learn about individualization through techniques custom-tailored to their own abilities and interests. Then they should use their knowledge in the in-service process in order to be able to transfer their learnings from the institute to the classroom.

The following sample outline of one institute that proved successful for intermediate grade teachers in four school districts includes a great deal of individualized work and on-location training for the participants.

Session

1. -Overview of planned emphasis; diagnostic test on individualization to determine participant's knowledge to date.
2. -Identification of each participant's curriculum preference for contract development.
    -Overview of innovative instructional techniques.
    -Independent work with tapes and recorder for securing in-depth knowledge of individualization, nongradedness or differentiated staffing, as they apply to personnel utilization and/or independent learning activities.
3. -In-depth discussion of the component parts of an individual contract and contract activity package (CAP), the development of appropriate diagnostic tests and "alternative learning materials."

-Independent work with tapes and identification of resources for developing CAPs.

4. -Demonstration of effective media to be employed with individualized programs of instruction.

5. -Introduction to behavioral objectives and their appropriateness to the contract and/or CAP.

6. -Independent work with tapes on behavioral objectives.
-Small-group discussions of the developing contracts and CAPs.

7. -Small-group discussions of developing contracts and CAPs.
-Independent work with tapes and films on behavioral objectives, individualization, nongradedness, etc.
-Instruction in the use of media in contracts.

8. -Each participant will submit his developed CAP.
-Small-group discussions of developing contracts and CAPs.
-Demonstration of CAP activities.

9-12. -Demonstrations of individualized instruction through the use of CAPs within the participating teachers' classrooms.
-Demonstrations will be held during school hours (morning and/or afternoon).
-The instructor, and as many of the institute participants who can obtain permission for released time, will observe.

13. -Large- and small-group discussions of the demonstrated individualized contracts and suggestions for improvement of submitted CAPs.

14. -Each participant will submit, in final form, a contract activity package, including charts, media to be utilized, materials, etc., suggested as learning multimedia resource alternatives for the students.
-Materials submitted will be accompanied by appropriate student directions for use, self-testing, etc.

15. -Display of instructional materials utilized in the development of contracts and CAPs for all interested participants. Explanations of CAPs and their development and utilization.
-Discussion of the development of advanced CAPs for future use.

It should be noted that each participant need not necessarily attend each session but may, with the consent and guidance of the instructor, elect to complete his assignments and studies in areas most conducive to his personal learning style. For example, a small group could conceivably meet in someone's home to listen to and analyze tapes and develop games, design contracts or be involved in other constructive work related to the institute's focus.

Tailoring Programs and Projects to Student Needs

A student's needs, interests and desires are products of his environment and aptitude, sensitivity and experiences, attitudes and opportunities.

There are many youngsters who learn happily and successfully in a structured, sequenced learning program, and the schools should provide that kind of environment for those who function well in it. Conversely, there are many other youngsters who require the time to explore leisurely without pressure and work out their own learning processes. Educators should provide options and that type of learning situation for them.

A student's needs can only be met by permitting sufficient variation in the school environment so that each child may select his own way of becoming involved with curriculum, life, learning and people. If we are to meet students' needs, we must help each student to choose wisely so that he may learn how to help himself to learn.

Once teachers realize that an individualized program provides many ways for children to acquire knowledge (structured and informal, predetermined and cooperatively developed by teacher and student, on-the-premises and off "campus"), it is much easier to meet each student's "needs" by tailoring a program that permits him a wide range of choice within the prescription that appears most suitable to his diagnosis.

Where a prescribed curriculum is used as a base for learning, the teacher may design a *curriculum* contract, but individualize the objectives, media resources, activities, interactions among students and instructional strategies, by permitting the student wide selection of everything but the curriculum topic (which can be modified in terms of his interests).

When the teacher has the latitude and support to develop individual curriculums on the basis of her diagnosis, independent contracts will provide the student with a totally individualized prescription.

If the students wish to select the curriculum cooperatively and then work on a group-identified topic ("sphere of interest"), the teacher can individualize the objectives, media resources, activities by which they will apply the knowledge they have gained, reporting methods and even the focus, if she believes these changes will provide a better learning experience for the students.

It is necessary to recognize that need and "relevance" may change as the student lives, grows, gains experience and interacts with others.

Because some students find it difficult to concentrate unless that which must be studied is interesting and important to them, the curriculum for any given youngster could be changing constantly. In addition, learning serves as a catalyst to ability, and knowledge invites expansion of the mind. A given individual curriculum may spiral outward constantly once a student has become involved in his own growth.

Rapid changes in a student's growth require constantly changing and improving objectives and media resources. The teacher who really individualizes instruction for her students may need to prescribe for only a relatively short time for some youngsters (one day, one month) and for a much longer period for others (one to two months). As students advance in their programs, they become increasingly independent, knowledgeable, mature, confident and proud of themselves. They feel less need for guidance, structure, conformity and peer-group approval and are able to progress rapidly with a reduced need for assistance.

As this process continues, it is appropriate to prescribe on a longer range basis for those students who are capable of sustaining interest, motivation and self-discipline.

A truly individualized program of instruction is personalized for a professional teacher as well as for the student. Given a flexible organizational pattern; time for diagnosis, prescription and individual conferences with students; extensive media; the skills of individualizing and the support of her peers and administration—the instructor will custom-tailor a program for each student so that learning *and* teaching blend into a dynamic process of growth for all concerned.

Teaming Teachers, Media Specialists, Librarians and Other Professionals to Meet Individual Student Needs

Within the past 10 years, part-time audiovisual teachers have been given additional responsibilities and redesignated as full-time media specialists; the out-of-the-way storage closet for the school's lone projector and three phonographs has expanded into a multimedia learning center; and the budget for textbooks has been reduced or supplemented with extensive appropriations for varied hardware and software items. To support this growth, district and/or regional workshops have been established to train teachers in the effective and creative utilization of media and equipment.

Not too long ago the school person in charge of audiovisual materials protected the machinery from teachers who might use it carelessly. Today, children in primary schools across the nation are using projectors, tape recorders, language masters, computers and other devices, formerly thought to be too complicated to operate except by thoroughly trained teachers or older students.

The days when teachers were requested to place their orders for a filmstrip "at least two weeks in advance" are behind us; today many of our classrooms are characterized by activity centers where children select equipment on the basis of their prediagnosed perceptual strengths and individual learning styles. Many districts have established instructional media centers and several have added dial-access systems that permit students to select their resources and obtain instant retrieval.

Within the short span of one decade, the role of media has changed from that of *supplement* to a *primary source* of instruction. Discussion of whether technology has aided in the revision of the teacher's role is academic; it has, and it will continue to act, as a catalyst to the rapidly changing and radically different teacher's function in the future.

As teachers intensify their exploration of instruction through individualization, it becomes very clear that a youngster must be initially diagnosed in terms of his academic achievement, potential ability, perceptual strengths, interests, motivation and self-discipline before a program of learning can be appropriately prescribed for him. Once accurate diagnosis is available and a prescription (course of study, program, unit assignment, contract, etc.) has been written, the student must be permitted to achieve his instructional objectives (the prescription) through *the media* with which he can most easily relate and that motivates and stimulates him to learn. This process of providing multiple media resources that can present information through a variety of perceptual avenues makes an individualized course of study possible for every student in our schools. Student selection of alternative multimedia learning activities will drastically change the future roles of both the classroom teacher and the media specialist as individualization spreads throughout our schools.

New Roles

When individualizing through multimedia, the role of the classroom teacher will alter from that of "transmitter of knowledge" to: (a) diagnostician of individuals, (b) prescriber of curriculum and (c) guide in the learning process. Similarly, the media specialist will no longer be the stockroom clerk or "supplier of what has been requested" (if it is available). Rather, he will be: (a) a diagnostician of curriculum, (b) a prescriber of resources and (c) a guide to the effective use of technology. The responsibilities of each will be so thoroughly interrelated that both will be required to complement each other's knowledge and plan jointly for the provision of prescriptions that can be mastered realistically by each student. Let us examine the process of interaction through which the media specialist and the teacher will cooperatively design the packaged prescription appropriate for each student.

Cooperative Designing

The teacher should diagnose each student to determine what he already knows, what he must still learn, what he would most like to learn and the media through which he finds learning most stimulating and rewarding for him. Although each child should be exposed to a wide variety of media to provide him with alternative ways of acquiring knowledge, it is important that the teachers recognize different learning styles. As indicated in Chapter 1, some children learn best through visual means, others through auditory means, still others tactually, some kinesthetically and most require reinforcement through multiple exposure to a variety of approaches.

After diagnosis, the teacher should outline either a short- or a long-term prescription of the instructional objectives that she, in her professional judgment, believes the child is capable of mastering. She should then discuss the objectives with the student (and, at times, his parents), and then add, delete, alter, accept or reject the prescription. When there is agreement by both the teacher and the student, the teacher should rewrite the instructional objectives into behavioral or performance terms, so that the youngster will clearly understand what he must learn, how he may demonstrate that he has learned it after he has and the degree of proficiency required of him.

At this stage the list of objectives should be submitted to the media specialist, who will examine it to determine the kinds and amount of software (pictures, study prints, films, filmstrips, slides, loops, tapes, records and programs) available for the student to select and use in meeting his instructional objectives. The media specialist should collate those media resources that are suitable to a given topic in folders so that the teacher may personally peruse the titles and descriptions and help select those that appear to be most appropriate for the individual student. Until such organization has been accomplished, it will be necessary for the media person to become thoroughly familiar with multimedia materials, the approximate reading and comprehension levels necessary for their effective use and the instructional relationship(s) that exists among the various materials. Obviously, other professionals, such as the librarian and psychologist, and support personnel (paraprofessionals, student teachers, typists, graphic artists, etc.), should be provided. Equally important is the allocation of time for design work, consultation, experimentation, etc.

Before the media specialist can ably determine the resources appropriate to a series of instructional objectives, he must be able to analyze the objectives in several categories:

1. Subject matter.
2. Level of in-depth study intended.
3. Approximate level of the student's comprehension.
4. Level of student's reading ability.
5. Student's major interests.
6. Student's learning style.

Once these factors are known, the media specialist should be able to prescribe appropriate media resources for the student.

The list of media resources should be categorized under the following subtitles:

1. Films
2. Filmstrips
3. Slides
4. Loops
5. Photographs
6. Study prints
7. Audio tapes
8. Video tapes
9. Records
10. Programs or packages
11. Books
12. Articles
13. Objects
14. Paintings, sketches, etc.
15. Places
16. Pamphlets and magazines

The media available under each category should be identified and the teacher alerted to the equipment necessary for the use of the software. If the student has had no prior experience with specifically required equipment, the media person (or a member of his trained student corps) should show the student how to use the materials and the equipment carefully. The student should use the media under supervision until he can proceed correctly and independently.

If the student cadres have not been taught to tutor their peers in the proper handling of software and hardware, paraprofessionals and/or volunteer parents should be trained to assume this responsibility.

With the advent of new instructional techniques like contracts which are specifically developed for the individualization of instruction, the use of media will continue to expand, so that, in a short time, learning will become more and more dependent on a multimedia approach. As this occurs, the role of the teacher will continue to become more professional and more specifically focused on the learning process; the role of the media specialist, on the other hand, will expand to include many of the important functions that will complement the teacher's changing and improved role. The media member of the team will be responsible for:

1. The diagnosis of perceptual strengths through the use of media as testing devices.
2. Curriculum suggestions on the basis of available materials and the student's perceptual diagnosis.
3. Supervision of student learning at a comprehensive instructional media center.
4. Translation of teaching ideas into graphic representation of the material to be learned.
5. Cooperative planning with the classroom teacher, the music, art, and gym teachers, the school librarian, psychologist and other support personnel.
6. Training of media (student, paraprofessional or parent) cadres to teach students to use media and to supervise the utilization of equipment and materials.
7. Serving as a resource person to students, parents and communities interested in enrichment programs beyond the completion of instructional objectives or school-based prescriptions.

The new partnership of teachers and media specialists will enhance the professional role of each as they seek to meet every youngster's instructional needs more effectively.

How can teachers begin the individualization process when their schools do not have the financial resources to either staff a media center or provide a media specialist to assist in the instructional process?

Student, parent or faculty teams should begin by cataloging what exists in the building. Either parents or faculty should assume the specialist role until additional staff can be employed. Students can be trained to operate and even repair equipment as part of their academic program. Media is interesting to many, and some retired persons in the community may be motivated by the opportunity to contribute to the educational process without the responsibility of direct supervision of youngsters.

Although the program may begin with the aid of volunteers, central office administrators, the board of education and the community should be apprised continually of the need for a professional media specialist. It is often easier to convince administrators of a need when the faculty demonstrates what it can do with limited staff and facilities, and then recommends an improved situation. Only a small minority is likely to accept effort, ingenuity and planning to improve the instruction of students, without being willing to demonstrate their appreciation through cooperation and the provision of necessary funds.

Reallocating Library Resources

The Walnut Hills Elementary School in Cherry Creek, Colorado, opened in September, 1969. This modern, open-spaced building contains three large learning centers instead of classrooms and an open-space "educational mall" filled with learning materials. The educational mall was the revitalized, modernized version of what, in traditional schools, would have been called "the library." The mall itself blends into the three learning centers but continues around the periphery of each with additional books and resource materials.[1]

This incorporation of what was formerly a centrally located accumulation of books and records into a mainstream of the learning environment represents one of the first genuine attempts in the nation to blend the best features of a library into a single, comprehensive and integrated total learning system. In terms of individualization, this is a way library materials may be used effectively by children on a continuous basis.

The dispersal of library resources among all of the learning areas of a building (whether they are "classrooms" or "centers") will affect the librarian and the way she functions.

The Librarian's New Role

As teachers begin to diagnose student needs and write individual prescriptions, they will need to be able to draw upon the librarian's

---

[1] *Differentiated Staffing in Schools* (Washington, D.C.: National School Public Relations Association, 1970), p. 18.

knowledge of available written and recorded materials that may be used to help children learn. Teachers will send student folders containing the prescribed objectives to the librarian who will identify those books, records, tapes, magazines, study prints, photographs and other items that may be listed as learning resources for the contract. The librarian will need to be aware of the reading and comprehension levels of the materials so that they may easily be used by the student. In addition, she should be available as a resource person for students who need assistance or who wish to continue their studies in greater depth than was originally prescribed.

In addition to keeping abreast of new materials and ordering inexpensive and expendable ones, the librarian will serve as a facilitator of the learning process by encouraging widespread reading, interage discussions of topics and less formality in the borrowing-take-home, keep-the-books-out policies.

The Contribution of Other Professional Personnel

The teachers of art, music, physical education, sewing, drama and other related areas may contribute to the development of the contract through suggestions of activities in their fields where the information that has been learned may be *applied*. The application of information, skills and concepts through interesting projects will help reinforce the results of the learning process.

The Difference Between Individualized and Independent Learning

When the teacher prescribes a course of study for a student based on her diagnosis of his abilities and needs, and then permits him many choices as to: (a) how he will learn what she has prescribed, (b) how he will reinforce and apply what he learns and (c) how he will share his learnings with others, the teacher has individualized that student's program.

It is possible to take predetermined segments of a curriculum and adapt or design them so that they become partially individualized for each student. This is the approach used in programed instruction, individually prescribed instruction, educational packages and curriculum contracts.

A totally individualized program, however, permits the teacher to design curriculum for and with each child that may be completely different from the curriculum prescription for other children in the same group. When this occurs, the child is working on an "independent" program, one that is completely different from the other prescriptions. In a sense, an independent approach can provide *total individualization*—a completely "personalized" learning experience.

All children in an individualized program work independently in that they assume the responsibility for their own learning and use the teacher as a resource consultant and guide. When children work on the same topic (curriculum, sphere of interest, unit, contract), they are working on an *individualized* program, if variations occur in objectives, resources and activities and in reporting selections. If, however, children are learning about vastly different self-designed areas (curriculums, spheres of interest, units or contracts), they are working on independent or fully individualized programs.

Six Techniques for Managing Your Classroom: Learning Stations, Interest Centers, Media Corners, Magic Carpets, Game Tables and Little Theaters

When children are learning through either independent or individualized programs, the learning environment should hum with activity and self-directed group interaction. The larger area (a classroom, a group of opened classrooms joined together, an instructional center or a learning laboratory) should be divided into many smaller ones. Children then may elect to work alone, with one or more peers in small groups or with the teacher or other resource persons.

The teacher moves among the students questioning, evaluating, responding, guiding and discussing concerns. As difficulties or deficiencies are recognized, she works closely with·the learner(s) to aid students in solving problems. Teacher-student conferences are held to determine how well the student is progressing and teach or reinforce (when necessary) items that need direct teacher involvement. As the teacher oversees the learning environment, the children direct themselves to work among the following learning areas.

Learning Stations

The development of educational "packages" made a wide range of sequenced programs available for classroom use and provided access to subject matter materials on different levels of difficulty. These resources, which permitted individual pacing as the student progressed through increasingly difficult levels of competency, led to a division of materials into organized segments. Teachers then developed "learning stations" where students could go to work on facts, concepts and skills. The stations include books, workbooks, tapes, films and other teacher-organized items related to a specific curriculum concern and level.

"Learning stations," then, are small areas or tables that house specific rated materials and resources related to a given curriculum, such as mathematics, language arts, science or social studies, at a particular level. For example, Learning Station 1 might have introductory, reinforcement, review materials and diagnostic, evaluative, terminal tests related to levels 1 and 2 in mathematics; whereas, Learning Station 2 would have similar materials in mathematics for levels 3 and 4—and so on. This arrangement could be duplicated in language arts or reading skills.

The station should be attractive, organized, numbered and well kept so that students can find the materials they require easily and with a minimum of frustration. Students should be cautioned to return materials to their correct place and category of difficulty when no longer in use. Color coding would aid in reducing any maintenance problem.

A learning station may consist of a table and shelves with accumulated materials where students select items and take them to their own desks (or another area), or it may include a table, desk, shelves and files for materials and some chairs or cushions for seating so that students may remain at the station to work. The materials on the level being served by the learning station should be interesting and varied and might include objects, items, books, magazines, programed materials or educational packages, workbooks, dittos, tapes, slides, films, filmstrips, photographs, cartridges, loops or study prints related to the selected curriculum and level, so that youngsters utilizing the station will find resources that they can understand and use.

Access to the station should be open. Students should be able to visit, take items to another section of the larger area (room or center) or remain at the station to work or discuss the topics with others.

When directions for usage, descriptions of the items and assignments for experimentation or provocative questions are attached to the materials, the learning station becomes structured. Some children prefer to handle materials without being required to go through prescribed procedures, experiences or reporting. These youngsters should be permitted the choice of using the learning station's resources as they prefer: (a) use of the station with responsibility for reporting (written or verbal); (b) examination of the materials out of curiosity, for reflection or for the purpose of learning without the responsibility of reporting; (c) use of the area for discussion purposes or (d) as a place to meditate, touch, examine and relax.

Individualization may encompass all of these procedures, from the more structured method that requires a given amount of reported or completed work each session to the less structured method that permits options in the station's use, providing the youngster shows interest, involvement and learning in some form. The latter process resembles some of the "open classroom" techniques being introduced across the country; the former procedure appears to be more acceptable to teachers approaching individualization through more structured classroom organizations. Neither approach is "right" or "wrong." Adopt the learning station approach that works best in your situation. Some students require structure, some will drive themselves relentlessly to complete every type of "assignment" they can find; others will adapt themselves to one form on certain days and select the other (or some variation) at other times; still others will respond to *any* procedure, while a minority may not respond to any approach.

Use the learning station as a beginning toward individualization. Motivated children will move forward quickly, regardless of the method they select or that you impose. The nonmotivated will progress more slowly, but may thrive with either learning station approach. Experiment, vary your methods, watch the students carefully and permit options so that they like the setting and feel comfortable in it. Give them time to find their own learning style; if it takes too long (two weeks), suggest a method for them and supervise their involvement. If one method does not work, try another after a given period (two weeks is a good experimental period). Keep introducing and testing new techniques until you have evidence that your diagnosis of a youngster's learning style is correct. If you suspect the child needs longer "adjustment" periods, proceed more slowly. There is no foolproof formula to motivate every student, but your professional expertise will assist you in recognizing what is working and what has failed for that student.

Interest Centers

A second small area where students may congregate to learn is called an "interest center." This section of the learning environment should house *interdisciplinary resources concerned with a selected theme* (topic, unit, contract) like pollution, brotherhood, transportation, racial conflict or dinosaurs. Here items related to *many curriculum areas* would be found, but they would be focused on one centralized sphere of interest.

In addition to the media resource materials related to the topic (objects, books, magazines, pictures, films, filmstrips, slides, cassettes, tapes, loops, cartridges, study prints, etc.), students might find: (a) assignment sheets (dittos or workbook-type pages); (b) small-group interactions (team learning, circles of knowledge, brainstorming, simulations, role playing, case studies and others) and (c) games (crossword puzzles, fill-in-the-missing-letter assignments, etc.), on which individuals or small groups might work.

Interest centers serve many purposes: (a) they are available as another option for students—an alternative way of obtaining information and concepts about a given topic; (b) they provide students with a means of gathering facts and broader concepts independently and (c) they build small-group activities into the learning process, to provide social interaction and group achievement. In this way, interest centers permit a teacher to begin individualizing while providing the students with a choice of either working independently or with one or more other students, because, although individualization is an important instructional goal, many youngsters prefer working with others—and, for them, isolated studying and learning may not be desirable. Indeed, even those students who seem to think best while working on independent units need others to interact with in order to test ideas and grow.

Media Corners

Most schools have limited equipment and must distribute their resources equitably among all the students in a given building. It is necessary, therefore, to provide each large group (30 to 35) of youngsters with enough "hardware" so that students may use the media equipment to obtain information, study concepts and develop skills. At the same time, it is inefficient and unnecessary to carry heavy equipment from place to place.

Some school districts have established multimedia instructional resource centers to house their films, filmstrips, "carousel," "opaque" and "overhead" projectors, screens, cartridge viewers, duplicators and other media equipment. In other schools this equipment is placed in various sections of the building, and students are permitted to leave their classrooms to use the equipment when appropriate.

Both methods of arranging media equipment have built-in drawbacks.

1. If students are to be free to use the equipment when it appears necessary or appropriate to them, they must also be free to leave their room (area) and go to the equipment in another section of the building. Since many students may need to be mobile at the same time, a constant traffic of incoming and outgoing students will exist. Unless the administration feels comfortable about an informal attendance procedure, it may be extremely difficult to keep tabs on students' whereabouts. Of greater importance, the "right time" may slip by or be greatly wasted in traveling to the media, or in waiting on lines.
2. The student leaves his teacher and peers to go to another area. His teacher cannot supervise or assist him; his peers (unless they join him) do not share his learning experience.

In preference (or in addition) to either the totally centralized multimedia instructional resource center or the partially centralized learning center, teachers may establish a "media corner" in each room (Photo 2-1). This area can house one overhead projector, one or two filmstrip machines, one super 8-mm cartridge viewer, one sound projector, three or four cassette tape recorders and many blank tapes. Additional equipment may be exchanged among clusters of three of four classes joined together as "learning pods" or media instructional areas (MIAs) when needed. The larger, more affluent media centers could be used as a library resource to provide special, needed media materials.

Students should be free to take software (filmstrips, film, tapes, slides, etc.) from either the interest center(s) or the learning station(s) to the media corner and use it there as a learning resource. The software should be replaced carefully when the student has finished using it. Cadres of students should form team task forces to assume the responsibility for demonstrating how to use, care for and organize the equipment and resources that complement it.

When one student begins to view materials, others are drawn into the procedure by interest, curiosity or social awareness. Students should be permitted to join each other in viewing, discussing, studying or applying the materials, provided each of the participants is receptive to the cooperative effort.

VERNON REGIONAL
JUNIOR COLLEGE LIBRARY

Photo 2-1. *Media corners containing a variety of learning materials and equipment should be established in every classroom. (Photograph courtesy of Amo DeBernardis, President, Portland Community College, Portland, Oregon.)*

Magic Carpets

Many youngsters concentrate and study best in a relaxed rather than in a formal atmosphere. Teachers have responded by introducing small pieces or remnants of carpeting (3' x 3' to 6' x 6') into learning areas. These, and other items, such as old blankets, pillows, cushions and discarded chairs or couches, have been placed in various sections of the room (area), and students are permitted to use them as places to study, congregate for discussions or work or relax before the next task.

One teacher called these areas "magic carpets" and told her students that "... when you relax on the magic carpets, ideas suddenly become clear and easy to understand!" Her pupils repeatedly verified that it really was easier to learn on a magic carpet than at a desk.

Magic carpets are excellent for small-group interactions, such as team learning, circles of knowledge, simulations or team task forces. They provide an intimate area for the social integration of work and reduce the feeling of pressure that many children tend to build up in a more structured setting. Youngsters can sit together, talk without interfering with other ongoing activities and share their thoughts or suggestions while simultaneously building a group camaraderie. Carpeted areas are also excellent for reading to one another and for student tutoring.

When using contracts to individualize instruction, students will have many opportunities to work independently, with one or two peers or in small groups of three to eight children. Having a place to work where the group can almost isolate itself from the larger group is conducive to developing interdependency and a strong sense of "community" among the participants. Contracts should include various small-group assignments and permit the youngsters choices for small-group completion.

Incidentally, magic carpets may "float" in a classroom or area that is already carpeted wall-to-wall!

Game Tables

Educational games are used extensively in schools today. Their major contributions to the learning process include: (a) introduction of a topic or concept; (b) application of information or concepts studies; (c) motivation and stimulation; (d) provision of an alternative teaching method or device; (e) opportunities for either individual or small-group focus on information through alternative media learning resources; (f) opportunities for independent concentration; (g) activities for small-group and/or interage interaction and shared experiences; (h) review or reinforcement of previously discussed or studied information; (i) remediation purposes and (j) opportunities for relaxation as a "break" in the school day.

Games are available for all age levels (preschool through adulthood), in all curriculum areas, and as interdisciplinary approaches to study. A repertory of these instructional devices aids in providing alternative resources, methods and activities for students and increases their options for learning.

Game tables should be available to students in different sections of the room (area, learning center) for use at appropriate times. When students have completed assignments, need or decide to use the games as media learning resources or activities or wish to relax for awhile, they should be able to go quietly to the table and select whatever is appropriate to their task or abilities. Games should be cataloged according to their level of difficulty or appropriate relationship to the curriculum. This task could be accomplished by listing those games that are appropriate to each student's comprehension or functional ability on the contract page that lists his "media resource alternatives." The student will then know which games he may choose and can exercise those options as he decides to do so.

When contracts list the use of educational games as possible resources, all the games included in the list should be available to the students. If games are suggested for relaxation rather than as curriculum supplements, the teacher could rotate their availability to maintain student interest and provide experiences with many possible choices.

Students need to be instructed in the use and care of games and all materials, and trained to replace them securely covered, with all parts returned, when they are no longer in use.

Little Theaters

Another area guaranteed to provide an exciting, dynamic learning atmosphere is called "the little theater"—an imaginative title for a creative and stimulating program. Here, in a section of the room that may be darkened or partitioned when necessary, students are free to become involved in a series of projects that require application of the information they have learned through the use of the media resource alternatives. Students are permitted to make slides, filmstrips, films, negatives, photographs, scenery props, costumes, backdrops for productions, rolled-paper "movies," multimedia presentations, transparencies, books and scrapbooks, and many other educational project materials related to drama, creativity and production.

These projects are, of course, appropriately related to the curriculum and/or contracts and provide application, review, reinforcement and synthesis of ideas for the students.

How to Know When You Have Succeeded: Self-Tests and Teacher Evaluations

Contrary to the evaluation system schools traditionally use—automatic group testing at the end of each unit or topic and, again, at the end of the term or year—contracts build in self-testing for a student as he progresses and teacher testing and guidance when the student indicates that he believes he has mastered his objectives.

Dwight Allen, dean of the University of Massachusetts School of Education, describes the "normal" learning curve as one that rises to a maximum point and gradually descends before the end of a given semester. The implication of this finding is that testing should not occur at the end of a term (period, year, semester) but, instead, should be employed at the point of maximum student growth. Each student's learning curve may differ radically from every other student's learning curve and should, therefore, determine when the student is evaluated. Indeed, some "end-of-term tests" should be given at the beginning of a course to aid in the diagnosis of each student.

Contracts build in self-evaluation assessments for students so that each learner may constantly test himself to: (a) determine what he learned while working on the contract, (b) find out what still remains to be mastered, (c) discover when he has completed his contracts and (d) evaluate the success with which he has mastered his objectives. Through this method, students will know how well they are doing and can determine for themselves when they should request the terminal teacher test. That final test could come at any point in the the sequence, whenever the student feels "ready" to demonstrate his knowledge of his contract objectives.

In this way both student and teacher participate in the student's evaluation, and testing occurs at the time of maximum retention, when the student feels most comfortable about what he has learned.

Chapter 4 describes in detail how to construct evaluation tests in relation to contract objectives.

II

Developing Contracts

3

Contracts: Placing the Responsibility for Learning Where It Belongs— With the Student

Learning by Contract: Definitions and Desirability as a Teaching Technique

A curriculum contract is a single unit or topic initially outlined by the teacher and selected from a predetermined course of study. It is expanded or restricted for use based on the teacher's diagnosis of each child's academic strengths, weaknesses and learning style.

A contract provides many opportunities for a student to learn independently and build on his potential abilities. As a result, the child begins to develop interest and pride in his accomplishments. Frustration and anxiety are minimized because the student is *given:*

1. An exact list of items that he must learn.
2. An exact method for showing the teacher that he has mastered the required learning.
3. A clear indication of how well he must do before he will be permitted to end one contract and begin another.
4. A choice of many media learning resources (tapes, records, films, books, pictures, single-concept loops, games, slides, etc.) on his academic level.
5. A choice of many activities through which information can be used and reinforced so that it becomes knowledge.
6. A choice of many ways in which he may share what he has learned with others (peers, teachers, younger or older children, etc.).

Children who are working on contracts actually learn how to

teach themselves and become independent learners, capable of progressing as quickly or slowly as their individual abilities permit. Motivation is increased because the youngsters are actively involved in the learning process by: (a) assessing their learning requirements; (b) selecting what they believe are appropriate resources and equipment; (c) choosing the activities in which they will engage to reinforce their learnings; (d) determining how they will share their knowledge with others; (e) assessing themselves; (f) deciding when they are ready to be teacher-tested and (g) contributing to the formulation of a subsequent contract.

Individual learning styles are identified and utilized effectively because youngsters are given the freedom of selection and will choose those methods of instruction with which they feel most comfortable, and also, they will pace themselves and change activities as they progress.

Success in contract learning is assured for motivated, self-disciplined children who want to learn. These students can focus on what they must learn, determine *how* they will learn, select reinforcement activities that appeal to them and display their achievements to others when they are ready. They need not be fearful that they: (a) cannot learn what the teacher requires; (b) will not learn as quickly as other children in the group; (c) will not score as well on tests, for they will be tested only when they believe they know the required information; (d) will not be able to complete the assignments—for they will select those assignments that are most compatible with their personal learning styles.

There is no single teaching technique that works effectively with every child, but curriculum contracts are a powerful means of helping the motivated, self-disciplined youngster (bright or slow) assume responsibility for his own learning. Through this method a bright or superior child can "fly" intellectually, while a slower youngster can learn the basic curriculum requirements with reduced pressure, more choice and deeper involvement in the learning process. Contracts also offer new hope of reaching nonmotivated, apathetic and "turned off" students, through their gradual acceptance of responsibility for learning that which is relevant to them in substance *and* process.

Moreover, the use of contracts, as outlined in this chapter, will tend to change teacher behavior as well as student attitude. Teachers will abandon reciting and lecturing once they observe that contracts generate student activity and self-motivated participation in the learning process.

Why Teach Through Contracts?

After years of teaching by means of traditional methods, teachers are now being advised to eliminate their former patterns and adopt new ones. If teachers (and their administrators and professors at schools of education) are to be convinced, the arguments for substituting contracts for lectures must be strong, clear and practical.

1. *Varied academic levels.* As indicated earlier, most teaching (kindergarten through graduate school) takes place by instructors *telling* information to groups of students.

When a speaker addresses an audience, the instruction must, of necessity, be geared to the academic level of the largest number of people present—but certainly not to individual levels.

In any group there are some who are academically "faster" and others who are "slower" than the "average." Some will become bored (certainly not challenged) by the simpler elements in the presentation that are necessary for those who are less bright. Others will become irritated by the repetition that is required for those who do not learn easily. In contrast, slower children will find the lecture comparatively complicated and too detailed to retain their attention. It is virtually impossible to address a group of 25 or 30 heterogeneously grouped youngsters on a curriculum topic and gear the content of each child's functional level at a pace that makes learning comfortable for every student.

In contrast to group lectures, a contract is written so that each child is able to operate on the academic level most suitable to him. He need not cope with either concepts or details that are inappropriate to his ability.

2. *Self-pacing.* When an instructor lectures, the audience can only absorb the content as quickly as the speaker delivers it. The speaker, in turn, can cover only as much territory as he believes the audience can assimilate at one time. In this way, both the lecturer and the audience are limited by each other's real and assumed restrictions.

An instructor who moves ahead too rapidly will lose the less able listener. If he proceeds at a painstaking pace that permits the slower youngsters to keep abreast, the more able students become restless and frustrated. If he varies his pace to provide interest, both groups are often sacrificed at one time or another during the presentation.

In contrast to group lectures, a contract permits individual pacing so that a student may learn as quickly or as slowly as he is able to move ahead. In addition, the student is neither embarrassed because others grasp the content more quickly than he, nor bored because he must wait for his peers to catch up to him academically before he is permitted to proceed. Each child works independently but may, by choice, team up with children who can pace themselves similarly.

3. *Independence.* When an instructor lectures to a group, the students can learn only what they hear or are required to read for the lecture. The children are dependent upon the teacher to bring information to them and clarify it so that each may learn what is required. Further, each student must learn the same thing to the same extent during a lecture and is required to participate in the same activities to reinforce his learnings.

Through the use of contracts, each child becomes personally responsible for learning what is required. He is given a choice of media resource alternatives, activity alternatives and reporting alternatives. The student may use varied instructional media to become acquainted with the information that the teacher wants him to absorb. Because of his exposure to a variety of resource materials, equipment and procedures, he will obtain a great deal of ancillary knowledge and learning tools, such as research skills, project development ability and interviewing techniques.

Moreover, the pupil quickly recognizes that the self-selection factor permits him to work in areas where he feels most comfortable. His self-pacing permits him to learn quickly, but well enough to retain what he has studied. As the child becomes accustomed to exercising freedom of choice and he assumes responsibility, he becomes increasingly independent of the teacher and/or specific learning materials such as a textbook. The student begins to recognize that he can learn as much or as quickly as he himself is able. He begins to take pride in his own accomplishments and utilizes the teacher as a guide and facilitator rather than as a fountain of knowledge from which he must sponge information.

A child who becomes an independent learner through the use of contracts will never again require or accept "spoon feeding" or narrowed restrictions in the learning environment.

4. *Reduced frustration and anxiety.* In an "average" class, every child is expected to complete the same amount of learning (the course of study) in the same amount of time (one school term or

year) with the same degree of attention and discipline. Each pupil is then graded in comparison with the other children in the class.

If one-third or one-fourth of the children in the class are rapid learners, let us consider child X "average" by contrast. That same youngster, when moved to another class on the same grade level, could appear to be "superior" if he is one of the brighter pupils in that group. Remove child X from the second class and place him in a third where most of the children learn easily and proceed at a faster rate, and he will be labeled "below grade level" or "slow."

These factors tend to create unnecessary pressure and tension for young children, who should experience pleasure from learning, not anxiety. When a youngster realizes that he will be marked not in terms of his own achievement but in comparison with how well his peers perform, he: (a) resents superior performance in others; (b) chastises himself (often unduly) for errors; (c) develops a poor self-image if he is not an outstanding performer; (d) loses confidence in his ability to earn good grades and often anticipates poor ones unjustifiably; (e) becomes anxious and strained; (f) seeks weaknesses in others; (g) may be tempted into cheating to earn "better" marks and (h) may become introspective and uncommunicative with family and teachers.

All this is in violation of good mental health guidelines and, in effect, tends to generate a self-defeating syndrome in which no one "wins." The child who scores poorly develops a poor opinion of himself; the one who does well develops a poor opinion of those who do not. He is also pressured to continue to do well to avoid the humiliation generated by failure. The high achiever in this climate may develop ego problems as a result of excessive competition; learning becomes secondary, grades primary.

Through the contract system, children are graded on three major bases—

1. Their achievement in terms of themselves:
   (a) Did they complete the contract?
   (b) Did they complete it within a reasonable amount of time?
   (c) Was the quality of achievement high?
   (d) What was the degree of proficiency with which they tested at completion of the contract?
   (e) Did they do more or less than was anticipated by the teacher?
   (f) Were they able to show behaviorally that they had learned what was required?
   (g) What was the quality of growth that each student achieved in comparison with his own previous level of performance?

2. Their achievement in terms of the group (class, grade) ranking:
   (a) Were they assigned a shortened, complete or lengthened contract?
   (b) Did most other children in their group perform as well, better or less well?
3. Their discipline in terms of the contract:
   (a) Were they usually self-disciplined?
   (b) Did they work well and permit others to work well?
   (c) Did they cooperate with the teachers and their peers?

A contract permits a child to "do his best" and be rewarded for his efforts, despite any innate relative difference among the students.

A youngster who actually belongs in the lower third of his group (class or grade) ranking who completed a shortened contract and learns what is required, can correctly be given an A for the first part of his grade. If he does well on the shortened contract but is operating on a fifth-grade, lower-third level, the second part of his grade could read 5^1. If he works diligently, applies himself, is self-disciplined, works well with others, has good manners, etc., the third part of his grade would be an A. Thus the "slow" child who functions at a lower-third-of-the-fifth-grade level, but who completed his contract effectively and demonstrates good decorum, could earn a grade like this:

Contract	Beginning Fifth	Self-Discipline
A	5^1	A

Consider the advantage of permitting each motivated, self-disciplined youngster to earn an A without jeopardizing "standards." The child is doing lower-third-of-the-fifth-grade work extremely well, and he is being rewarded for his effort and achievement—not punished for his lack of native intelligence or ability. Moreover, these concepts could be utilized in multiage or ungraded levels and in the new organizational patterns in which analytical narrative comments replace the A's and B's.

Contracts permit children to function at their maximum potential without creating artificial competition. They are rewarded for what they accomplish and how well-behaved they are, not for the personal intelligence potential with which they were born and for which they are not necessarily responsible. "Acceptable" behavior should include effective participation and appropriate learning interaction—not rows of silently conforming children.

5. *Interests.* In most classrooms, children must follow a pre-

scribed curriculum; each child learns the same thing at the same time in the same way.

Through contracts, the teacher may recognize that individual children have specific interests and/or talents. Limitations imposed by student load and schedules may prevent the teacher from working with all pupils on a one-to-one basis, but the instructor *can* develop an *independent* contract (see Chapter 4, "Creating Independent Contracts") for individuals who: (a) academically or psychologically are not able to cope with regular curriculum contracts, (b) are so far advanced that they require special contracts or (c) have completed the regular curriculum contracts and are ready for newer and wider horizons.

Contracts permit selected youngsters to study in depth those areas that are most enticing to them and cultivate their interests toward the maximum of their potential.

The very nature of contracts appeals to students' interests because the choice of resource, activity and reporting alternatives motivates children to select those materials and activities that are most stimulating, tempting or exciting to them.

6. *The nonreader.* When a teacher either lectures or explains something to a class, the children are exposed to the information only once—unless they can read. If they have not absorbed everything or most of what was said, they must resort to reading the information and directions or they will be unable to fill in the gaps between what they must learn or do and what they could not remember or understand.

Children who cannot read are penalized in the ordinary classroom, for they cannot hope to learn as quickly or as much as their peers who are able to read. In fact, the gap between readers and nonreaders often widens as the successful students are spurred on to new heights by the personal satisfaction of their achievements, while the losers become more despondent and apathetic.

Contracts provide students with alternative ways of learning (media resource alternatives) information. A child who cannot read well may use pictures, films, slides, records, tapes, single-concept loops, games or a multitude of other materials to learn and achieve.

The child who can read, on the other hand, finds reinforcement stimulating through the wealth of learning alternatives that are available to him with a contract. Effective learning requires frequency, intensity and variety. A contract provides all three through extensive availability of multimedia.

Designing Curriculum Contracts

A curriculum contract should include:

1. Behavioral objectives written *for the child* that explain:
   (a) What the child must learn.
   (b) How the child can demonstrate that he has learned the specified information, applications, skills, etc.
   (c) The degree of proficiency expected of the child.
2. Media resource alternatives.
3. Activity alternatives.
4. Reporting alternatives.

Including and Identifying Instructional Objectives

We all remember the anxiety we personally have experienced in "studying" for a test. We would look through our books or notes attempting to guess which questions the teacher would ask. Most of us reviewed our materials by trying to anticipate what the most important things to remember might be.

Why should students have to *guess* what the teacher believes is important or necessary for them to learn? Doesn't it make much more sense for children to be *told* what they have to learn? Once they are aware of what they must learn, they can more easily focus on acquiring that information or skill. *What* the child must learn is called his "instructional objective." It is a statement describing one of your educational intents.[1]

The purpose of including instructional objectives in a contract is twofold: (a) to assist the teacher in analyzing and determining what the minimum specific learnings for a given topic or unit must be and (b) to provide the student with a clearly itemized listing of what he must try to learn.

Identifying instructional objectives is a relatively uncomplicated task:

1. Identify the curriculum topic (or unit) to be studied.
2. Divide the topic into broad subcategories.
3. Determine the essentials that must be learned in each of the sub-

---

[1]Robert F. Mager, *Preparing Instructional Objectives* (Palo Alto, California: Fearon, 1962), pp. 1-2.

categories. The number of essentials, of course, may vary extensively among the subcategories.

4. List the essentials for each of the subcategories in order of importance. The most important items will become the minimum essentials of the contract and will be required of every child who undertakes to learn through the contract method. The remaining items will be required of those children who show the ability to work extensively on an independent basis. The number of items included in each child's contract varies—dependent on the child's academic ability in the curriculum area of the contract, his motivation and his self-discipline.

5. Combine the minimum essentials for each of the subcategories into one list. Number the items on the combined list.

6. Formulate a second list by combining all of the essentials (including the minimum essentials) into one list. Number all the items on the combined list. You now have two separate lists—one that contains only the minimum essentials of the topic and one that contains all the essentials of the topic. The list of combined minimum essentials constitutes the minimum instructional objectives for the contract. The total list of combined essentials (including minimum essentials) constitutes the overall instructional objectives for the same contract.

The exact number of instructional objectives may vary among curriculum contracts on the same topic. A "slower" child receiving a contract on India, for example, should have fewer instructional objectives assigned to him than a "faster" child. Since the instructional objectives have been itemized in the order of their relative importance, it is simple to assign "only the first six objectives" or "the first 13 objectives" as the teacher diagnoses the potential ability of each individual youngster to work independently at the task of learning the required information (Figure 3-1).

Translating Instructional Objectives into Behavioral Objectives

If the pupil is to be given a list of what he must learn (his instructional objectives), he must also be told how he can show the teacher that he has mastered these objectives once he has done so.

We should not ask the child to *know* what "karma" is (the anthropology of India), for he will not clearly understand how he can prove that he knows what the word means unless we indicate a method for demonstrating that he has mastered that knowledge. Instead, we must select a means whereby he can indicate his knowledge of the meaning of karma.

DESIGNING CURRICULUM CONTRACTS

IDENTIFY

   Topic ➡ India

   Subcategories ➘ Anthropology Geography Politics
                     Economics   History   Sociology

   Behavioral Objectives

          Media
   Resource Alternatives

   Activity Alternatives

   Reporting Alternatives

Figure 3-1

We have several alternatives at our disposal. We might suggest:

1. From a list of several definitions, be able to circle the correct description of karma; or
2. Be able to write a one-sentence (or one-paragraph) description of karma; or
3. Be able to tape-record your definition of karma; or
4. Write a short composition explaining the meaning of karma and add your opinion of this Indian belief; or
5. Write a short poem explaining the Indian belief of karma; or
6. Develop a series of photographs or drawings to illustrate the meaning of karma; or
7. Combine any of the suggestions or develop your own assignment to explain karma

When instructional objectives are written so that a student understands how he will be called upon to demonstrate that he personally has accomplished them, the objectives are called *behavioral objectives,* because the youngster, through *performance* or *behavior,* can verify that he has achieved what his teacher has required.

An excellent analysis and description of how to prepare instructional objectives expressed behaviorally (in performance terms) is found in Mager's book *Preparing Instructional Objectives.* The reader is carefully taken through each step of development and is taught to understand and write instructional objectives, so that children will know how to evidence what they have learned. He points out that "To describe terminal behavior (what the learner will be *doing*):

(a) Identify and name the overall behavior act.
(b) Define the important conditions under which the behavior is to occur . . .
(c) Define the criterion of acceptable performance."[2]

Once a teacher has utilized these sound directions, writing behaviorally stated instructional objectives is not difficult. The only caution we would like to offer is that Mager's objectives are written for adults and, particularly in the elementary grades, teachers must write objectives *to* and *for* their pupils. Thus, rather than writing the objective as Mager indicates, "Given a list of 35 chemical elements, the learner must be able to recall and write the valences of at least 30,"[3] it is suggested that teachers reconstruct the objectives so that

---

[2]Mager, *loc. cit.,* p. 53.

[3]*Ibid.,* p. 30.

Examples of the Process of Identifying Instructional Objectives

Possible Curriculum Topics for Contracts

Possible Broad Categories

Wind	Use of Capital Letters	The Concept of Numeral Four	Shapes	India
identification	recognition	addition	identification	anthropology
uses	application	subtraction	construction	sociology
control		division	uses	politics
		multiplication		history
				geography

The Essentials

Wind	Use of Capital Letters	The Concept of Numeral Four	Shapes	India
Identification	*Recognition*	*Addition*	*Identification*	*Anthropology*
What is it? How do we know it's near?	Know the capital form of all 26 alphabetical letters. Be able to write all 26 alphabetical letters in their capital forms.	Be able to add all combinations of 4 and 1, 2, 3, 4, 5, 6, 7, 8 and 9.	Recognize circles, squares and triangles. Find circles, squares and triangles in common classroom items. Identify circles, squares and triangles in items outside the classroom. Be able to describe circles, squares and triangles.	Know what "karma" is. Know what the caste system is. Understand the following nouns: Brahmin, Kshtriya, Vaishya, Sudra, minority, Hinduism.
Uses	*Application*	*Subtraction*	*Construction*	*Sociology*
What does it do? How does it help us? How does it hinder us?	When do we use capital letters? Proper nouns. Beginning of sentences. What is a "proper noun"?	Be able to take 4 away from 5, 6, 7, 8 and 9.	Draw a circle, a square and a triangle.	Know what the "joint family system" is. Who makes decisions? Where do younger siblings live? What is a dowry? Who commands the most respect in an Indian family? What part do children play?
Control		*Division*		
Why should we want to control the wind? Can we control the wind? If so, how?		Be able to divide 8 and 12 by 4.		
		Multiplication		
		Be able to multiply 4 x 2 and 4 x 3.		

Uses

Use circles, squares and triangles in drawing common items.

Politics

Who was Mahatma Gandhi?
What does "Mahatma" mean?
How did Gandhi dress when like an Indian peasant?
When did he dress like an English gentleman? Why?
What has his attitude toward "foreign rule"?
Was he "for" or "against" Europeans?
Know the meaning of the following terms: civil disobedience, equality, "Quit India," low jobs, nonviolence.
What do the colors of the Indian flag mean?
What is the meaning of the symbol on the Indian flag?
Who was Jawaharlal Nehru?
How did Nehru's philosophy differ from Gandhi's?
Who is Indira Gandhi?
Is she related to Nehru or to Gandhi?
Is sex or age more important in India?

History

What is the main religion in India?
What other religions exist in India?
When was Christianity introduced into India and by whom?

91

Examples of the Process of Identifying Instructional Objectives

Possible Curriculum Topics for Contracts

The Essentials

History

When was Judaism in introduced into India and why?

Who was St. Thomas?

Know the following names: Dravidians, Aryans, Prince Guatama, Buddhism, King Asoka, Buddha, Zoroaster, philanthropist, Moslem, Sikh.

Geography

What is the name of the enormous mountain range in northern India?

Name two or three Indian rivers.

What is the monsoon?

What are the climates of India?

Why does the Deccan Plateau not get heavy rainfall?

Name some of the crops grown in India.

Subcategory Essentials in Order of Importance

Wind	Use of Capital Letters	The Concept of Numeral Four	Shapes	India
What is the wind?	Recognize the capital forms of all 26 alphabetical letters.	Be able to add all combinations of 4 and 1, 2, 3, 4 and 5. (Ditto pages 1-11 as needed.)	Recognize circles.	Explain what the caste system is.
What does it do?	Be able to write all 26 capital letters.	Be able to take 4 away from 5, 6, 7, 8 and 9. (Ditto pages 40-55 as needed.)	Recognize squares.	Explain what the joint family system is.
How does it help us?	When do we use capital letters?	Be able to add all combinations of 4 and 6 and 7. (Ditto pages 12-15 as needed.)	Recognize triangles.	Identify Mahatma Gandhi.
How does it hinder us?	What is a noun?	Be able to add all combinations of 4 and 8 and 9. (Ditto pages 16-23 as needed.)	Identify circles.	Identify Indira Gandhi.
Why should we want to control the wind?	What is a proper noun?	Be able to divide 8 and 12 by 4. (Ditto pages 60-69 as needed.)	Identify squares.	Describe the monsoon.
Can we control the wind? If so, how?	What is a complete sentence?	Be able to multiply 4 x 2 and 4 x 3. (Ditto pages 89-100 as needed.)	Identify triangles.	Name some of the crops grown in India.
	Use capital letters correctly (proper nouns, beginnings of sentences).		Draw circles.	Explain "karma."
			Draw squares.	Describe a dowry.
			Draw triangles.	Who commands the most respect in an Indian family?
			Find circles, squares and triangles in common classroom items.	Is sex or age more important in India?
			Find circles, squares and triangles in items outside the classroom.	What is the main religion in India?
			Be able to describe circles, squares and triangles.	What other religions exist in India?
			Use circles, squares and triangles in drawing common items.	What is the enormous mountain range in northern India?
				What are the climates of India?
				Explain the following nouns: Brahmin, Kshatriya, Vaishya, Sudra, minority, Hinduism.
				Who makes decisions in an Indian family?
				Where do younger siblings live?
				What part do children play?

Subcategory Essentials in Order of Importance

Wind	Use of Capital Letters	The Concept of Numeral Four	Shapes	India
				What does "Mahatma" mean?
				How did Gandhi dress when like an Indian peasant?
				How did he dress when like an English gentleman? Why?
				Name two or three Indian rivers.
				Why does the Deccan Plateau not get heavy rainfall?
				What was Gandhi's attitude toward foreign rule?
				Explain the meaning of the following terms: civil disobedience, equality, "Quit India," low jobs, nonviolence.
				What do the colors of the Indian flag mean?
				What is the meaning of the symbol on the Indian flag?
				Who was Jawaharlal Nehru?
				How did Nehru's philosophy differ from Gandhi's?
				Is Indira Gandhi related to Nehru or to Gandhi?
				When was Christianity introduced into India and by whom?
				When was Judaism introduced into India and why?
				Who was St. Thomas?
				Explain the following names: Dravidians, Aryans, Prince Guatama, Buddhism, King Asoka, Buddha, Zoroaster, philanthropist, Moslem, Sikh.

94

they are clearly written at the student's level of verbal comprehension. The revised objectives might read: "You will be given a list of 35 chemicals to memorize. You must be able to remember at least 30 of the chemicals and be able to write their valences." Also, where Mager uses the phrase "the learner" (". . . the learner must be able to. . .") substitute the word "you." Your behaviorally stated objectives will therefore read: "You will be able to. . ." or "Be able to. . ." This procedure is much more personal to a youngster and suggests a direct psychological link between what the teacher wants him to learn and how he can show her that he has learned it.

Defining the Required Degree of Proficiency for Students

"The degree of proficiency" sets goals of quantity, quality, accuracy or some other standard for the behavioral objectives you will require the child to master. Will you be satisfied if a slower child learns only 15 of the 20 spelling words assigned for the topic, or, because you have already taken into consideration that he may not be able to learn as many words as a brighter child, and have, therefore, assigned him fewer words, actually expect him to learn all of the 20 assigned words?

This is an area where the professional "diagnosis" of the teacher must be considered and followed. There are several ways of coping with this problem:

Traditional Method	*Contract Method*	*Alternate Contract Method*
The teacher assigns 20 spelling words per week to every child in the class, regardless of ability.	The teacher develops a list of appropriate words for the contract topic. The list varies in number (20 to 120 if necessary), depending upon what is relevant and may need to be used in reading and writing activities related to the contract.	The teacher develops a list of appropriate words for the contract topic. The list includes *all* of the words which she believes the youngsters should learn in order to participate effectively in the contract.
The slower child cannot learn 20 words in one week and is therefore defeated before he begins. This approach "builds failure" into the schools.		The slower child, the average child and the faster learning child are all given the same long list. Each is told that these are the words related to the contract but that each child should learn as many and whichever words on the list that he can.
The average child may be able to learn 20 words in one week, but the process will require a great deal more effort on his part than for the faster youngster.	The slower child is given a spelling list composed of the minimum essentials on the total spelling list. If he succeeds* with these during a given time period (may be three days or more), his list is expanded to include more of the words on the total list. If he is unsuccessful,	The level of expectation must vary, dependent upon the teacher's perception of each child, but in this way,
The faster child can easily learn the 20 words		

_____

* See footnotes on page 97.

Traditional Method

(he might also be able to learn 30 or 40) but is not challenged by the process. In addition, the exercises that the teacher requires of all the children ("write each word three times" or "use each word in a sentence") are not necessary for this pupil, who, as a result, becomes either irritated or bored.

With this method, the individual child's academic ability, rate, style of learning and motivational level are not considered in either the diagnosis or prescription for learning.

Contract Method

he is given fewer words during the following study interval. Experimentation continues until the teacher can accurately estimate the number of new words the learner can successfully master in the given amount of time, and this time span may vary for each youngster at different periods during the year (or day).

The average child is given a spelling list composed of more of the minimum essentials on the total spelling list than were given to the slower child. If he succeeds with these, his list is expanded in subsequent study intervals to include more words. Words are added (four to six at a time) until he is either unsuccessful or showing irritation or stress.

The faster child is given the total spelling list of minimum and maximum essentials. He is expected to learn a reasonable number of words, 20 to 40, in a given study interval (three days to one week). If he learns all of the words accurately, he should be given the freedom of learning his next list of words as he chooses without required exercises, drill or activities. If he is unsuccessful with the number originally given, the number of words on the list should be reduced by four or six during the next study interval. Experimentation with the correct number of words assigned should continue until the teacher can accurately estimate the number of new words the learner can successfully master in a given amount of time. Changes in ability and rate of learning should be noted and used.

Alternate Contract Method

a child is not necessarily limited by either the teacher's perceptions or the choice of words selected for his "group." Frequently children may find "difficult" words easier to master than "easy" words.

If the contract is planned as a three-week (or more) unit the teacher might assess each child's spelling growth once each week by saying† each of the words on the total list and permitting each child to write those words that have been learned during that study interval. Children will learn different words, but as long as they are learning words on the list, the teacher should accept their efforts (within the minimum number of words prescribed) as successful.

With this method, the individual child's academic ability, rate and style of learning and motivational level become an integral part of the learning process.

When the child is self-motivated, he becomes self-disciplined too and achieves at an accelerated rate.

Traditional Method	*Contract Method*	*Alternate Contract Method*
	Permitting children to learn a list of spelling words in the manner most comfortable for them aids children in acquiring knowledge through their own individual learning styles. Some children need to focus on a word visually and mentally repeat it to learn its spelling. Others need to write it once or hear it spelled by a classmate before the word is mastered. Still others must experience visual, auditory and tactile repetition or use within sentences.	
	With this method, the individual child's academic ability, rate and style of learning can become an integral part of the learning process. The teacher becomes a facilitator of the learning process; he or she is then truly a professional diagnostician, prescriber, guide and assessor for new teaching-learning decisions.	

Whichever method you select to use to determine the child's required degree of proficiency, be certain that you have diagnosed his ability to achieve as accurately as possible. When you indicate to a youngster that you expect him to achieve 85% or better, realize that anything less than 85% will be self-depreciating to the pupil. Establish a degree of proficiency that is reasonable (in terms of the child's ability to learn and retain), and that will help the child recognize his own success when it is obtained.

As a general guideline, if you limit the number of behavioral objectives that the child must master and permit him choices as to how he will achieve his objectives, the youngster is more likely to

---

*"Success" is defined in terms of the degree of proficiency expected of each child. A teacher may tell a slower child, "I expect you to be able to spell every word on your list correctly by next Monday." This youngster's list might include only eight words. The teacher may have the same expectations for another child whom she knows is a faster learner, but the second child's list could include 25 words. The level of expectation should always be high (85% or better), but the amount of learning that must occur should vary with the child's academic ability, rate of learning, self-discipline, motivation and learning style.

+The teacher need only tape-record the entire contract spelling list once. It can then be played back to the group (or individual) as frequently as is necessary or desirable.

reach the degree of proficiency established for him. Further, establish teaching-learning "partnerships" with each student so that at least some of the contracts are designed jointly. Relevance and achievement will increase through this type of collective involvement.

Defining Media Resource Alternatives

Multimedia resource alternatives include the multiple ways of learning information that are available to children today.

Years ago, much knowledge was acquired through two basic methods—listening to teachers or reading books. With the advent of radio, students began to listen to that medium, and when television became available, it drew children for longer and longer periods of time as a medium that provides information as well as entertainment. In recent years, educators have begun to incorporate all media into the instructional process, and many school systems today boast of "media resource centers"[4] in their district.

Media, to be used effectively, must be easily accessible to the children and should be placed in each classroom. Many administrators bemoan the sad fate of an unused number of overhead and opaque projectors, screens and carousel slide projectors that gather dust in closets and storage areas in the basements of schools. In turn, teachers complain of the inavailability and unaccessibility of equipment that must be ordered well in advance, is kept under lock and key and which, when in need of repair, is out of use for extended periods of time.

If the modern classroom, or learning center, is to produce a positive learning environment, it must be stocked with extensive resource alternatives (materials and media equipment) readily available to children, so that they may learn through a variety of instructional sources. This approach is essential because children (and adults) have different perceptual strengths and weaknesses as they begin to learn. Some students learn easily by listening, others must rely on their visual experiences and still others require intensive tactile involvement. For most children (particularly the very young), learning is generally acquired through a *combination* of perceptual

---

[4]For practical recommendations on establishing and using media resources, see Kenneth J. Dunn and Jack Tanzman, *Using Instructional Media Effectively* (New York: Parker Publishing Company, Inc., 1971).

exposures that are frequently repeated in different sequences and with appropriate timing and intensity.

When children listen to someone speaking (or to a record or tape), the information is being received through one sense only—hearing.

When children read a book (or look at pictures), the information is being received through one sense only—seeing.

When a combination of media is incorporated into the learning process, learning occurs more easily and quickly. The greater the number of senses involved in acquiring knowledge, the higher the retention of knowledge is likely to be.

When a child watches a film (or slides) and listens to the narration, the information is being received through two media—sight and sound (Photo 3-1).

Photo 3-1. *Some students learn best through visual experiences. (Bell & Howell, Audio-Visual Products Division, Chicago, Illinois.)*

When a child writes letters in the sand (or with water on the chalkboard), the information is being received through two media—sight and touch. If a record plays the "Alphabet Song" (or directions for forming the letters) at the same time, a third dimension is added—sound.

One of the major reasons for utilizing media resource alternatives in the learning process is to provide children with opportunities to capitalize on their individual perceptual strengths through multiple sensory ways of learning.

Further, the use of a wide variety of equipment and materials to introduce and then reinforce information provides the "frequency, variety and intensity" that produces effective learning.

A third reason for including media resource alternatives in contracts and contract activity packages permits choice—children are not structured into artificial learning boxes, wherein every child must learn the same material in the same amount of time with the same level of interest and attention. The child may choose how he will master his instructional objectives. He develops a stake in the learning process, for his selection of resources places the responsibility for learning squarely where the responsibility lies—on his shoulders (Photo 3-2). The student must select wisely or he will experience difficulty. He may change his resources and experiment with another resource, but he will lose time. If time is not a factor, the child may test several alternative resources before he recognizes those with which he is most successful. Eliminating time limits or allowing reasonable time ranges is desirable because the pupil then learns how he can most easily acquire knowledge in a relatively less pressured manner. If learning becomes an enjoyable experience for him, he is much more likely to seek additional self-determined contracts and resources in an ever increasing positive cycle.

Guidelines for Multimedia Resource Alternatives

Teachers in urban or rural areas may believe that suburban school systems are better equipped to begin individualized programs, but machines and materials alone do not improve instruction. Indeed, there are many filmstrips, transparencies, tapes and projectors and players gathering dust in well-stocked media centers. Few classrooms or learning groups in any area now have *all* the equipment necessary for implementing effective contracts.

Individualization is a new way of *behaving* for both teacher and student. Media is a strong tool to aid the process but is not essential to begin. Once involved, teachers, students and administrators will find the means to improve their media resources.

For example, all classrooms can gradually develop an extensive collection of media resource alternatives by obtaining the money for

Photo 3-2. *Students develop a stake in the instructional process when they select the resources through which they will learn. (Bell & Howell, Audio-Visual Products Division, Chicago, Illinois.)*

basic equipment and materials from textbook and teaching aid allocations, if it is not available as an addition to the budget.[5] Teachers who wish to individualize instruction would undoubtedly be willing to exchange some of their workbooks, textbooks, supplies and other items for basic equipment and materials.

Moreover, some of the best work in individualization to date has occurred in disadvantaged areas in Los Angeles, California (student film program), Philadelphia, Pennsylvania (Parkway School), Newton, Massachusetts (self-designed instruction) and Freeport, New York (St. John's University teacher training project), where little media was available.

---

[5] *Ibid.*, p. 47.

Finally, more and more foundation and state and federal funding have been shifted to urban centers, and much of it would aid instruction if used to train teachers and provide media resources for individualization.

The following list may serve as a guideline for the number and types of multimedia resources that lend positive support to contract activity packages. Central media resource centers and libraries should be tapped to provide other needed resources.

Media Equipment and Materials for a Group of 30 Pupils

Required Media Resource Alternatives	*Ideal Media Resource Alternatives*
1 part-time district graphics technician to develop transparencies and other materials for the teacher	1 full-time school graphics technician to develop transparencies for teachers and children (with the teacher's prior approval)
1 overhead projector	2 overhead projectors
1 opaque projector for every two groups of 30 pupils	1 opaque projector
1 cassette recorder for every 10 children and one for the teacher	1 cassette recorder for every child and one for the teacher
1 cassette tape for every child (to be erased and reused)	6 cassette tapes for every child (may be saved, reused, erased or retaped as needed)
6 books (definitely not sets) on varied levels for each contract topic being studied for each child in the class (may be shared and varied)	12-15 books on varied levels for each contract being studied for each child in the class (may be shared and varied)
2-3 films or filmstrips on the contract topic	6 or more films, film loops and filmstrips on the contract topic
2 teacher-made or commercial tapes on the contract topic, at different levels	6 teacher-made and selected commercial tapes on the contract topic, at different levels
1 listening post set	4 listening post sets
1 carousel projector for every two groups of 30 pupils	2 carousel projectors

multiple booklets, articles, tapes, records, slides, and pictures (captioned) on each contract topic with multileveled explanations clipped to them

multiple educational games on the contract topic, each with varied levels of required ability

Media Equipment and Materials (Cont'd.)

as many sequenced sets of good slides or filmstrips on the contract topic as are available (minimum—one)

several sets of varied-level dittos to serve as either introductory or reinforcement activities for the contract topic

extensive arts and crafts materials, including colored mounting paper, felt and other cloth material, wood, metal, plastics, construction paper, tissue paper, paints, crayons, colored pencils, magic markers, clips, staplers (and staples), transparent tape, brushes, clay, plaster of paris, plasticized modeling materials, cloth, thread, needles, binding tape, cardboard for covers and jackets, lightweight leather in attractive colors and every other type of substance that could be utilized effectively in terms of fulfilling contract activity alternatives (see "Defining Media Resource Alternatives," this chapter).

If children are to become independent learners, they must have resources (other than the teacher) through which they can acquire information.

Once the information has been acquired, it should be reinforced frequently and in a variety of ways to insure retention and potential application. Media resource alternatives, therefore, must include several different types of equipment and materials to provide listening, seeing and tactile experiences for youngsters. The wealthier the supply of resources available. the more enriched the contract activity program will be.

During the summer of 1970, 60 graduate students at St. John's University in Jamaica, New York, undertook to develop contract activity packages for prefirst and prekindergarten pupils in Freeport, New York. Little equipment was available for use because what did exist in the district was being used by the classroom teachers with their regularly scheduled classes. The graduate students developed their own media resource alternatives (tapes, games, pictures, stories, transparencies, etc.), and these were used with ease and success by very young children who had not had prior experiences working independently. These "teacher developed" resources proved to be as effective as any commercially produced materials.

Teachers cannot be expected to develop original media resource alternatives for each of 30 pupils in a group, but a combination of currently exisiting equipment and materials, in conjunction with what can be produced through cooperative efforts of teachers, aides, parents, student teachers and older students, makes the use of resource alternatives a realistic possibility for today's schools.

The Importance of Activity Alternatives

Children will be acquiring information through multiple resource alternatives. Once they have been exposed to the contract topic materials and have begun to achieve their instructional objectives, opportunities must exist for further development and reinforcement of the learning so that it becomes knowledge and can be successfully retained and applied in new situations.

Activity alternatives are a series of educationally sound steps, procedures, projects or assignments in which the youngster can participate. Each of the activities represents an educationally sound method for using and reinforcing what is being learned by the child.

An extensive list of possible activities should be developed by the teacher for the children engaged in contract learning. The items should be: (a) given to the children in written form and (b) mounted attractively on a chart for display in the classroom. The list should include at least 20 different alternatives, but *each child should be permitted to select those activities in which he will participate.*

Dependent upon the teacher's estimate of the child's potential ability to complete activity alternatives independently, the teacher should assign a *number* of activities to each youngster. (Richard is bright and self-motivated and probably can complete at least five different concurrent projects successfully. James is an "average" youngster, but he has a long attention span. He is likely to complete at least three activities effectively. Fred, however, is academically "slow." He wants to learn but has just recently become able to stay with a single assignment for an extended period of time. Perhaps Fred should be assigned one project initially. If he completes that one, has enjoyed the process and does well on his instructional objectives, the teacher may increase the number of projects for which Fred will be responsible in subsequent contracts.)

In all cases, however, the teacher merely indicates the *number* of activity alternatives that each child should complete. The child determines the specific activity alternatives that he will pursue.

The advantages of providing the student with a choice in the selection of activity alternatives are many:

1. Motivation is increased because the youngster has participated and declared "ownership" in determining how he will learn and reinforce his learnings.
2. Interest and attention spans are increased and boredom reduced

because selection is based on what appeals to the child (Photos 3-3, 3-4 and 3-5).

3. Enjoyment is more likely to result because the pupil will choose those activities with which he feels most comfortable and which he is able to complete.
4. Successful completion is much more feasible because the pupil is free to select those activities that are possible for him to complete successfully on his level of comprehension and performance.
5. Abilities will be enhanced and the student will be more eager to experiment with other activities as he is exposed to media and the developing and completed projects of his peers.
6. Self-assessment and decision-making effectiveness will improve. When a child selects a project that is too difficult for him, he soon recognizes that he has made an incorrect decision. He is permitted to change his selection and choose one in which he can function with more ease. The experience will then help him to learn how to assess future projects (or problems) according to a more realistic evaluation of his own abilities. This recycling activity can provide the youngster with excellent growth opportunities to exercise and correct his judgment, make decisions, appraise situations and develop alternative procedures.

Sharing Knowledge Through Reporting Alternatives

Once the child has achieved his instructional objectives and reinforced his knowledge through activity alternatives, the final step in the contract involves sharing with others the information he has acquired.

By discussing, depicting or writing about acquired knowledge, the student is required to synthesize and focus his thinking so that it can be expressed succinctly and in sufficient detail for adequate explanation and communication to others. This process becomes a secondary form of reinforcement for the pupil who is providing the information. Learning to express knowledge clearly and interestingly is a skill that will be required over and over again in school and throughout life.

The exchange of information and resulting discussions, reactions and interrelationships tend to stimulate interest in related phases of the topic and broaden involvement in new areas of learning. Pupils begin to build a reservoir of knowledge gained through the reporting procedure, and most of them feel a strong sense of pride and accomplishment in displaying that they have completed their instructional objectives successfully (Photo 3-6). Contributing and sharing enhance both individual and group learning.

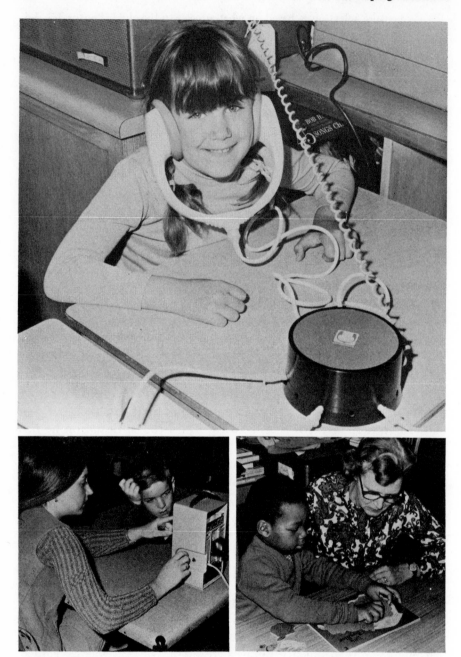

Photos 3-3, 3-4 and 3-5. *Interest and attention spans increase and boredom is reduced through student selection of learning activities. (Photographs courtesy of Freeport Public Schools, Freeport, New York.)*

Photo 3-6. *Students feel a strong sense of pride and accomplishment when they can demonstrate that they have completed their instructional objectives successfully. (Photograph courtesy of Freeport Public Schools, Freeport, New York.)*

As with activity alternatives, the student is given a comprehensive list of alternative reporting possibilities and is assigned only a *number* of those of his choice to be completed. Each child is also permitted to select the methods that he will use to share his findings with others.

A Sample Contract

Africa

Introduction

1. This contract is for an interage class of intellectually gifted elementary children.
2. The unit on Africa might take between six and eight weeks.
3. Almost all of the children would receive Behavioral Objectives 1 through 10. The exceptions would be those children who evidenced difficulty as the work progressed.
4. The brightest children would receive Behavioral Objectives 1 through 15. Flexibility is built into a program of this nature in that any child

not "labeled" brightest in the original assessment could also be given additional objectives if he completed the others and showed interest in continuing.

Behavioral Objectives

1. Given an outline map, you will be able to write the following names directly onto the map in their correct locations:

   (a) Africa   (e) South America (i) Mediterranean Sea
   (b) Europe   (f) Australia   (j) Red Sea
   (c) Asia   (g) Atlantic Ocean (k) Gulf of Aden
   (d) North America   (h) Indian Ocean   (l) Gulf of Guinea

   You must correctly locate items (a) through (h). If all 12 items are right, you will show your superior knowledge!
2. You will be required to fill in correctly the names of at least 12 African countries in blank spaces on an outline map of Africa.
3. You will be able to write two short paragraphs telling: (a) what a missionary is and (b) how the missionaries affected the lives of inhabitants. You will succeed *only* if your paragraphs answer the questions *what* and *how*.
4. You will be able to list at least three great states, nations or empires that existed in Africa hundreds of years ago.
5. You will describe the experiences of: (a) at least three explorers of Africa, (b) at least three countries that gained their independence from colonial powers and (c) at least three colonial powers that were ousted from control in Africa.
6. You will be able to list at least three mineral resources that are found in abundance in Africa.
7. You will be able to list at least two animals that live on *each* of the following terrains: (a) deserts, (b) rain forests, (c) savanna.
8. You will be able to match the names of different types of African people with paragraphs that describe their physical characteristics, the areas where they live or their way of life. You will pass if you have three correct. More than three correct makes you something of an expert!
9. You will be able to complete a five-question True or False examination on social organization in Africa. Three correct answers will be acceptable; but I dare you to get all five right!
10. You will be able to list at least five African tribes.
11. You will be able to write brief answers to three questions about diseases in Africa. At least two of these questions must be answered correctly.
12. You will be able to write an essay on how the topography (physical features), climate and rainfall of at least one kind of area affects the lives of the people who live there.

13. You will be able to tape a 2-minute talk on the African arts (dancing, music, sculpture, etc.). Your talk must include the ways in which they are used in African life.
14. You will be able to tape a talk about religion in Africa. You *may* include something about the Christian or Moslem religions, but you *must* include the facts you know about "traditional" African religions.
15. You will be able to relate how Africa has influenced life and culture in the United States and one other part of the world.

Media Resource Alternatives

Filmstrips

42930–	Africa, The Land of Developing Countries
129 –	Union of South Africa
356 –	Bantu Peoples
647 –	Lagos–Federation of Nigeria
657 –	How People Live in Africa
659 –	The Congo Basin
661 –	Southern Africa
662 –	The Eastern Highlands (Africa)
663 –	West Central Lowlands (Africa)
664 –	The Nile Valley

Transparencies

AEVAC– Physical, Social and Economic Geography of Africa
AEVAC– Political Geography and Nationalism of Africa
Africa– United Transparencies, Inc., Binghamton

7081– Physical Features
7082– Climate and Vegetation
7083– Races in Africa
7084– Important Tribes
7085– Early African Kingdoms
7086– Colonialism I
7087– Colonialism II
7088– Colonialism III
7089– Agriculture and Mineral Products
7091– African Diseases
7092– Independence I
7093– Independence II
7094– Independence III
7096– Literacy
7097– Urbanization
7098– African Religions

8809.41 Western Africa

8809.42 Northeastern Africa
8809.43 Central Africa

159—Africa: Mineral Resources
169—Africa: 1900-1967
170—Africa: 1967

Motion Picture Films

429.85 — Oasis
*5.4   — African Continent: An Introduction
*5.411 — African Continent: Northern Region
*5.413 — African Continent: Southern Region
*5.415 — African Continent: Tropical Region
          *Available through Central Loan Collection
          —African Village Life in Mali-International Film Foundation

Slides

Social and Historical Relationships Between Tribes
Art of Central Africa—Distributed by Prothmann Associates

Study Prints

Children of Africa—Society for Visual Education

Pictorial Material

Early African Civilization—D.C.A. Educational Products

Books (Available in school library)

Glubok, S. *The Art of Africa*
Dobler & Brown. *Great Rulers of the African Past*
Levy, M. *Caravan from Timbuktu*
Gatti and Attilio. *New Africa*
Hughes. *First Book of Africa*
Sutton. *Illustrated Book About Africa*
Woodson. *African Heroes and Heroines*
Newman, M. *Africa's Animals*
Griffin, E. *Continent in a Hurry*

Hall, O. *Quest. With Stanley in Africa*
Lauber, P. *Congo River into Central Africa*
Whitney, P. *Secret of the Tiger's Eye*
Kenworthy, L. *Profile of Kenya*
Joy, C. *Getting to Know Tanganyika*
Dubois, W. P. *Otto in Africa*
Frank, F. *My Friend in Africa*
Davidson, B. *Guide to African History*
Vlahos. *African Beginnings*
Caldwell, J. *Let's Visit Middle Africa*
Mirsky, R. *Thirty-One Brothers and Sisters*
Dietz, B. *Musical Instruments of Africa*
Joy, C. *Getting to Know the Sahara*

(Available in public libraries)

Luthuli, A. *Let My People Go*
Kaye, G. *Great Day in Ghana*
Schatz, L. *Bola and the Oba's Drummers*
Schloat, W. *Duee, A Boy of Liberia*
Stein, M. *Majola, A Zulu Boy*
Newrath, M. and Worboys, E. *They Lived Like This in Ancient Africa*
Pine, T. and Levine, J. *The Africans Knew*
Sweeting, E. *African History*
Bleeker, S. *The Ashanti of Ghana*
"   *The Masai*
"   *The Pygmies*
Borten, H. *The Jungle*
Bernheim. *From Bush to City*
Gunther. *Meet South Africa*
Kittler, G. *Let's Travel in Nigeria and Ghana*
Williams. *Africa: Her History, Lands and People*

(Available in class)

Greig, M. *How People Live in Africa*
Ben-Jochannan, Brooks and Webb. *Africa: The Land, the People, the Culture*

(Read chart from left to right)

Activity Alternatives

Select at least_____of the following activities.

1. Write a letter to another child, pretending you are a boy or girl in one of the African tribes.

2. Write a script for a radio or television program on which an African who has become a slave is being interviewed.

3. Make a travel poster advertising a safari in Africa.

4. Write a travel pamphlet about a trip to the part of Africa you found most interesting.

5. Make up a crossword puzzle using new words and information you have learned.

6. Prepare a museum display on any aspect of African art.

7. Develop commentaries for a filmstrip or a slide showing.

8. Dress paper dolls as some of the people you have learned about.

9. Make up a quiz to give your class.

10. Write the commentary for a radio or television program on African music and instruments. Try to borrow a recording of African music and/or any African instruments.

11. Write a letter to the United Nations asking for any materials on a country in Africa that you especially liked studying.

12. Keep a make-believe diary about your experiences in one of the countries studied.

13. Make an attractive jacket describing information you have learned for a book on the topic.

14. Prepare a travel lecture.

Reporting Alternatives

1. Read your letter to a small group of students. Tell the children that they may ask you any questions that they would include in a letter if you were "pen pals." Be prepared to answer their questions.

2. Produce and present the program.

3. Display the poster and persuade the children to "sign up" for the safari.

4. Pass the pamphlet around and be prepared to answer questions about the trip you are advertising.

5. Stencil the crossword puzzle and let other students try to complete it.

6. Display the objects (or pictures of them) for your classmates. Pretend you are the museum guide and give a brief lecture about what you are showing them.

7. Present the filmstrip and slides with your commentary to a group of children.

8. Display the dolls and prepare a 2-minute talk about them.

9. Permit several pupils to try to take the quiz. Be certain you have the correct answers written on an answer sheet for them.

10. Produce and present your program.

11. Display the materials to a group of children. Be prepared to tell them why you chose this country to "investigate" more thoroughly, and how the materials you secured added to your information or pleasure.

12. Combine the experiences into a "book" entitled "My Autobiography" and show it to your teacher, your principal and a group of your classmates. Add your book to the resource alternatives available for study of your topic.

13. Display the jacket and prepare a 2-minute talk describing the book.

14. Give the travel lecture before a small group of classmates. You may also tape-record it for future use for others who are working on the same topic.

15. Write an original story describing the information you most enjoyed learning.

16. Write a letter to a friend recommending that he study this topic too, and explain why.

17. Make a scrapbook of African art and sculpture.

18. Make a map on which you print brief information that you have gathered.

19. Write questions you think everyone should be able to answer on the topic. Organize a panel participation program.

20. Make a tape for a classmate, telling why she ought to learn more about the topic.

21. Make a mural to illustrate the information you consider interesting.

22. Prepare an illustrated "weather report" of the area you studied.

23. Write a letter to an imaginary friend about fictitious travels concerned with your topic.

24. Write a script for a radio or television program about any aspect of the topic (i.e., slavery, colonialism, nationalism).

25. Visit a museum or the Afro Arts Cultural Centre (222 West 13th Street, New York City).

26. Make a product map of Africa.

27. Learn how to say something in Swahili.

Chart (*Cont.*)

15. Permit others to read your story. Ask them to tell you what they liked best about it. They may write their comments on a separate sheet of paper that you may attach to the end of the story.

16. Send the letter.

17. Display the scrapbook.

18. Display the map and answer questions about it.

19. Present the panel participation program to a small group in class.

20. Ask one or two classmates to listen to the tape and tell you whether they have become interested in the topic.

21. Display the mural and answer questions that may arise.

22. Give the report to three or four other children.

23. Mount and display the letter.

24. Produce and present your program.

25. Tell a few of your classmates about your visit.

26. Display your map. Tell the children what the map shows and be prepared to answer questions.

27. Tell the children what you have learned to say in Swahili and be prepared to tell them what role this language has played in communication between peoples who speak different tribal languages.

Contract Prepared by Gladys Lavine
New York City Public Schools

Figure 3-2

Contract Summary

1. The teacher must first develop a series of instructional objectives or goals for her group.
2. The instructor then determines which objectives can be achieved by each student.
3. Each student understands how he can demonstrate that he has achieved these instructional objectives when they are assigned to him in self-performance terms as behavioral objectives.
4. The learner then begins to acquire the required information or concepts through a variety of media resource alternatives (equipment and materials).
5. He reinforces his learning through self-selected activity alternatives (projects that require information review, use, translation and synthesis).
6. The student then shares what he has learned with others through a variety of self-selected reporting alternatives.

4

Developing Contract
Activity Packages

Expanding Contracts into Contract Activity Packages (CAPs)

When an initial diagnostic test, a self-test and a terminal assessment are added to the basic contract, the contract becomes a contract activity package or CAP. (See Figure 4-1.)

Diagnosis prior to prescription of a contract may be made through administration of either a standardized achievement test or a teacher-developed test. An informal analysis of the youngster's comprehension and knowledge of a specific topic may be sufficient at the start.

Diagnosis prior to contract design will determine:

1. What the pupil already knows about the contract topic in order to avoid unnecessary repetition.
2. What the pupil still must learn about the contract topic, so that the teacher can design his behavioral objectives.
3. What the pupil's academic achievement to date has been in order to prescribe the length and complexity of the contract.
4. What the pupil's learning style is in order to design the contract according to his present level of motivation, attention span, perceptual strengths (visual, auditory, tactile), self-discipline, persistence and self-esteem.
5. What the pupil's major interests, skills, talents or problems are.

Once the teacher has an accurate, comprehensive profile of the child, she will be better able to design a contract. The teacher-facilitator can now better estimate how many behavioral objectives this particular student should probably be assigned, the kind of media resource alternatives from which he will probably be best able to learn and the kinds of activity alternatives with which he will probably achieve success. Should the youngster elect to participate in activity alternatives that are inappropriate for him, the teacher should not redirect him at first but, rather, permit him to attempt to complete the contract according to his selection. The child must learn for himself what is most appropriate to his current operational ability.

After diagnosis of the youngster's strengths and weaknesses, the teacher should prescribe that portion of the curriculum contract that she believes the student can complete successfully. Obviously, the instructor may prescribe the entire contract, a shortened or elongated version or a variation. The contract that is then given to the pupil should include behavioral objectives (instructional objectives written in performance terms), media resource alternatives (the many materials and equipment from which he can learn), activity alternatives (the projects for reinforcement) and reporting alternatives (ways in which he can share what he has learned). In addition, the contract should include a self-test.

The Self-Test

Attached to each contract activity package should be a short test that the child administers to himself whenever he believes that he has mastered his contract objectives. He can, without anxiety, take the test that the teacher developed in relation to the behavioral objectives included in his contract. For example:

Behavioral Objective

Self-Test

1. You will be able to write a short paragraph describing the joint family system. You will include information about what happens when the eldest son marries, where his younger siblings live and where his younger sister lives when she marries.

Write a short paragraph describing the joint family system. Include information about:
(a) What happens when the eldest son marries.
(b) Where the eldest son's siblings live.
(c) Where his younger sister lives when she marries.

Figure 4-1

2. You will be able to examine a series of nouns and, with complete accuracy, draw a line between each noun and its correct definition. The nouns will include:

With 100% accuracy, draw a line from each numbered noun to its correct definition.

Mahatma Gandhi	Ganges	1. Ganges	mountains
Indira Gandhi	Hinduism	2. Hinduism	winds
monsoon	Dravidians	3. Himalayas	first main religion
Himalayas	Aryans	4. monsoon	Aryans
Buddha	Prince Guatama	5. Dravidians	first civilized people
Brahmins	karma	6. invaders	a river
"Quit India"	Sudras	7. Buddha	Prince Guatama
	Harijans	8. Brahmins	an elite minority
		9. Sudras	the lowest caste
		10. rebirth	karma
		11. Mahatma Gandhi	Indian leader who brought about independence from the British
		12. Indira Gandhi	Children of God
		13. Harijans	Indian slogan
		14. "Quit India"	First woman prime minister

When the child has completed the self-test, he should ask the teacher for the correction sheet on which the answers are noted. He may mark the test himself, noting which of his objectives he has mastered and which he still must learn. The child need not reveal this grade to his teacher. He should have the option of re-examining the media resource alternatives in order to fulfill the required behavioral objectives. At this point the child will be aware of his gaps in learning, and he should continue to focus on the uncompleted objectives. When the student is certain that he has mastered the remaining objectives, he should return to the teacher and request the terminal test.

Terminal Assessment

After the pupil has taken and graded his own self-test, returned to the resource alternatives to study the unfulfilled objectives further and then believes that he has now learned all of the instructional objectives in his contract, the teacher will administer the final end-of-contract examination. This test would include the questions usually given at the completion of a unit, topic, course of study or period, so that the teacher and student will know what the child has and has not mastered. The content of the terminal assessment is identical to the material in the self-test administered by the child. The testing procedures should reflect the behaviors described in the contract behavioral objectives.

It is suggested that the same instrument may be used as both a student self-assessment and the terminal assessment. The student has focused on learning the objectives, he has prepared himself for the test by using a blank test to continually assess himself and when he believes that he is ready, the teacher seats him near her desk (or in a quiet area of the room) and administers the test to determine whether he has actually mastered the contract content. He has prepared himself, is familiar with the questions and, if broad concepts and related facts are the major portion of the examination, he may demonstrate his understandings and knowledge. Most students will be successful, and that is another valuable advantage of using contracts.

Enrichment or Review Materials

Should a child who has satisfactorily completed a contract express continued interest in the contract material beyond the behavioral objective requirements, the teacher may prescribe additional different, more complex or varied objectives and media resource alternatives to permit the student to probe deeper or more extensively into his area of interest.

Should a student who has satisfactorily completed a simplified or shortened contract express interest in attempting a longer contract, the teacher may prescribe such a contract in the next assignment.

Should a child who has completed a contract and scored lower than 85% but higher than 70% on the terminal assessment indicate that he likes learning through contracts, the teacher could assign: (a) fewer behavioral objectives or (b) fewer and less complex behavioral objectives in the succeeding contract. She might also require that the pupil review the contract media resource alternatives and attempt self-improvement before assigning a new contract.

Children who score less than 80% on a contract terminal

assessment may require different teaching strategies to achieve their contract objectives and should not be assigned additional contracts unless the 80% or lower grade they received represents an academic improvement over former grades and a performance level *at or above the level predicted by the teacher in her original diagnosis.*

Contract Activity Package (CAP) Summary

A contract activity package includes:

1. A diagnostic test.
2. Behavioral objectives written for the child.
3. Media resource alternatives (books, records, films, tapes, games, slides, etc.).
4. Activity alternatives (independent or group projects—see "Contract Activity Alternatives," Chapter 3).
5. Reporting alternatives (see "Contract Reporting Alternatives," Chapter 3).
6. Self-assessment test.
7. Terminal teacher assessment.
    If necessary:
8. Media resource alternatives review.
9. Enrichment objectives.

Creating Independent Contracts: Capitalizing on Interests and Special Abilities, Differences in Content

In any group of 30 youngsters, there are several with unique problems who would profit from a different type of curriculum in addition to varied kinds of instruction. For these children, a basic "curriculum contract" designed around the usual course of study would be inappropriate. Contracts designed to meet the specific needs of individual children who require an interest-centered curriculum are called "independent contracts" because they are developed *independent* of the required basic curriculum.

Examples of Children Who Require Independent Contracts

Case Study 1

Clayton Barnes is "educationally disadvantaged." He reads three years below his anticipated nine-years-of-age grade level, his math skills are poor and he "hates" school, teachers and tests. Clay has been called "unreachable" and "unteachable" by educators who, literally, could neither reach nor teach him.

Clay has one area of susceptibility—he loves animals. His eyes well up with tears at the sight of a wounded or suffering creature. (This empathy does not extend itself to humans.) He exhibits endless patience with stray or abandoned mongrels and once nurtured a near-dead bird back to excellent health. He often requests information about animal anatomy and explains that he must know "so I can fix the poor thing."

One of the ways to help Clayton Barnes want to learn how to read would be through the development of an independent contract based upon the troubled boy's concern for and love of animals. A great deal of scientific knowledge would be necessary to provide Clay with the information he needs and wants. Most elementary school teachers would not have this type of background. Resource persons, such as science teachers, the school physician, the school nurse, the librarian, professionals in the community and local college faculty, might be able to provide appropriate resources or specific background. Clay's teacher would then have to simplify the pertinent concepts, facts and skills so that they could be easily comprehended by the youngster.

Because there are probably few texts, tapes, films or records for elementary school children on how to care for animals medically, resources based upon the simple care and nurture of animals could be used for their illustrative qualities, and the teacher could develop a narrative tape (with a cassette recorder) to accompany the more complex media resource alternatives that do exist.

The topic would be different from those of the usual curriculum topics, but the instructional strategies would be the same. Having gathered all the information possible about animal medicine and care, the teacher should try to determine which concepts and details might be most interesting to Clay. (She might even ask him!) From among those selected, she should attempt to simplify the material at a level suitable to Clay's ability to comprehend, absorb and utilize. The results of her selection and translation of material into understandable items should then become Clay's instructional objectives. These should be written in performance terms so that Clay will know how to show the teacher that he has mastered the information.

The instructional techniques used with the resource, activity and reporting alternatives for this independent contract should be identical with those used for curriculum contracts. The only difference between this independent contract and a curriculum contract is that the subject matter deviates from the required course of study because, in this case, the course of study is completely alien to the child's interests and Clay is unable to function academically without intense internal motivation.

It might be argued that: (a) teachers do not have the time (or inclination) to develop independent contracts for individual children or that (b) children should conform to the overall strategy employed for classes or groups. Unless children who deviate from the "average" are motivated, they may not learn. Each year that passes without educational growth widens the gap between where students should be academically and the achievement to which they can realistically aspire. Once a child like Clay begins to obtain the information he *wants* and can recognize his success in the learning process, he will undoubtedly continue to desire additional knowledge and skills.

Teachers who try to motivate children toward curriculum contracts are progressing positively, for it is necessary to encourage, excite, entice and involve children in their own learning. But not all children can become motivated by something outside themselves, and for these, independent contracts are essential.

Case Study 2

> Trudy Johnson is so disturbed that she is unable to function in an average classroom for more than 20 minutes before she begins to amble around the room, touch objects, annoy classmates and prevent the teacher from continuing the lesson. The school psychologist believes that her condition is not severe enough to permit placement in a special school. Trudy remains in her class until the disturbance becomes intolerable to the instructor, then the child is transferred to any one of the other classes at her grade level with understanding teachers who will accept her for only short periods of time.
>
> If Trudy is to be helped to learn, she must have the guidance and attention of trained specialists who can knowledgeably direct and channel her energies and abilities. If she is permitted to continue in her present pattern without personal assistance, her behavior will undoubtedly be viewed as negative and remediation may be impossible. If the necessary elementary school specialists are not available for Trudy, a teacher or group of teachers must pool their interests and skills in aiding Trudy to participate, for her own future self-esteem and growth.

Designing an independent contract for Trudy is more difficult than developing one for Clayton Barnes. Trudy has: (a) a short attention span, (b) no cohesiveness with a group, (c) a need for interaction with other children, (d) a need for tactile experiences, (e) no specific topic in which she is personally interested and (f) little (if any) ability to listen to a teacher lecture or direct.

When attempting to identify an appropriate contract topic for Trudy, the teacher must provide a series of activities which do not require that Trudy continue to work without stopping, changing, varying or terminating; she should have the option of returning to study or review these projects when she is "ready" to do so.

The teacher should also provide many opportunities for Trudy to work with and learn from her peers (the many reporting alternatives should be adapted so that they become either activity alternatives or media resource alternatives appropriate to her learning style). Trudy may not be able to listen to or look at materials or media for any length of time and may have to learn from interactions with other children; if this is true, team learning, simulations, learning circles and role-playing would be excellent teaching techniques to build into her contract. She also needs many resource and activity alternatives which include the use of tactile experiences and short "team" activities so that she need not function alone and can begin to feel like "part of" a group.

The specific topic may not be important in Trudy's case. It is possible that a regular curriculum contract would be acceptable if the resources, activities and reporting alternatives included essentially tactile and group experiences. To the extent that Trudy's contract is different from the curriculum contract awarded to other children in her class, it becomes an independent contract for her.

Case Study 3

> Francine Mace is a sixth-grade student who comprehends more intricate mathematics than any teacher in the elementary school that she attends. Last year her teacher recommended that Fran be permitted to "regroup" for math, and the principal permitted Fran's mother to taxi her to the local junior high school for "enrichment work" two mornings each week. The practice could be continued, but the math teacher in the junior high school believes Fran is so advanced that she should be permitted to take advanced studies in appropriate classes on a full-time arrangement. Fran is an all-round fine student, and she says that she really loves math and has asked for permission to learn about computers and mathematical theories.

Obviously, this precocious youngster should not be restrained until her peers reach her level of academic ability. An independent contract can be developed for Francine so that she may continue to progress as rapidly as her potential permits. If it is decided to permit her to advance her mathematical abilities and interests, her teacher will probably require assistance in constructing an appropriate and challenging contract for Fran. A mathematics curriculum coordinator, high school teacher or college instructor could lend assistance, and it might be appropriate to seek guidance from either industrial or governmental agencies.

The age-old concern that some teachers raise ("If she learns intermediate and high school math now, what will she learn when she reaches high school?") is totally inappropriate if we believe that the school's responsibility is to help each child reach his maximum potential. If teachers restrict (and we should be encouraging) superior youngsters from advancing more rapidly than the "average" children, we are, in fact, stifling talented and intellectual students. Schools should free children to ". . . be nobody but themselves in a world which is doing its best, night and day, to make them everybody else . . ."[1]

This is part of the purpose and promise of education; the use of independent contracts will free children to be themselves, pursue topics of interest and learn in a manner that is uniquely theirs.

Using Different Contract Designs

This chapter has described the method of teaching through the use of contracts. The design of contracts will vary, of course, depending upon the age and ability levels of the students for whom they are being written. Younger and slower youngsters require more precisely written objectives and procedures (although the inclusion of alternatives in media resources, activities and reporting is a necessity for all). With older, more mature, motivated and/or self-disciplined students, the contract design may provide for increased flexibility, enrichment, student-determined objectives or, in some cases, total development by the student with permission and guidance from the teacher.

The suggestions for contract development are guidelines to the custom-tailored design work that must fit and match the prospective consumer—the student.

------

[1] E. E. Cummings; paraphrase of a letter written in 1955.

How to Begin

The following procedures detail the entire sequential process involved in contract development. The first time a teacher develops a curriculum or independent contract, the process may seem long or tedious. For this reason, a small group of teachers who work with students on a similar learning level should cooperate in constructing their initial contracts. Subsequent contracts require fewer hours of effort, and soon the teacher will find that contract development is no more difficult than lesson plan writing. Contracts are far more effective, however, and will reward both teacher and student with increased productivity and enjoyment of the teaching-learning process. Moreover, teachers and entire schools will find a massive teaching resource file of contracts available for individualizing instruction at all levels soon after the process begins.

Basic Steps in Contract Development

1. Analyze the contract topic to be developed.
2. Divide the topic into major subcategories (usually four to eight groupings) and identify the important concepts and facts that should be learned.
3. Using the subcategories as a base, construct instructional objectives for the concepts and facts that should be learned.
4. Rewrite the instructional objectives in behavioral terms so that the student will know how he will be tested on each instructional objective.
5. Construct test items for each of the instructional objectives developed.
6. Identify which instructional objectives *must be mastered* by all students, *should be mastered* if possible, *would be an asset* to the students and would be considered *ancillary* or *enrichment* learnings. Combine all of the behavioral objectives into one list, placing the "most" important objectives first, those which "should" be mastered second and so on, placing the enrichment concepts last.
7. Determine where the cutting-off place will be for the slower children, the "average" child, the more advanced youngster and the exceptionally bright. (All children in a group should *not* receive the same length contract. The slower youngster should receive a shortened version—only the "most important" objectives or only *some* of the "most important" objectives, depending upon his ability to work independently and comprehend without intense teacher-pupil interaction. As the child's motivation and self-discipline increase, the contract he is assigned may be lengthened.)

8. Locate resource materials through which the behavioral objectives of the contract may be learned. Itemize the accumulated resources into a list of "contract learning alternatives." Duplicate this list for the students.

9. Develop a list of "contract activity alternatives" from which pupils may select a series of projects or assignments to use and apply the information they have learned. Duplicate this list for the students.

10. Develop a related list of "contract reporting alternatives" through which pupils may share and reinforce their acquired learnings. Duplicate this list for the students.

11. Design a pretest using the test items previously prepared.

12. Establish and explain "standards of performance" to the students. (Five correct answers out of six may indicate understanding of the objective. Eight out of ten on a criterion check should indicate understanding.)

13. Give the pretest to students. Record objectives needed by each student.

14. Have each student keep his own record of objectives.

15. Assign students to small-group or individual instruction based on pretest results.

16. A self-test may be used to further refine groupings. The self-test may be used for regrouping after certain vocabulary has been taught; it may provide evaluation for a student's personal progress; it may be used as a measure of pupil performance.

17. Instruct individuals and small groups of pupils in their areas of weakness. Large-group instruction is only appropriate when introducing a topic in which the levels of pupil information are essentially similar.

18. Teacher's planning begins again with Step 1 for the new unit of work to follow.

19. Give the pretest for the next unit of instruction.

20. Conduct a posttest on the unit being taught. (The posttest can be exactly the same as the pretest.)

21. Record objectives not yet mastered by individual students.

22. Make provisions for re-exposure to media resource alternatives or reteaching these objectives immediately. You may also incorporate them into the next unit of teaching.

23. Evaluate the number of objectives mastered. Determine: (a) whether the student is capable of learning through contracts; (b) whether he should be assigned the next one and (c) the appropriate length of the next contract to be assigned to this student (if any).

Variations at Different Levels

As indicated in the beginning of this section on contract design, teachers may vary contracts according to their perceptions of the ability of their students to learn through a more or less structured series of procedures. This chapter has established guidelines for developing curriculum and independent contracts for students and was devised to serve as an introduction to the development of contracts. The creative teacher, however, should not be restricted by a pre-established set of rules that might possibly serve to inhibit her ingenuity and initiative.

A Sample Contract Activity Package

This is a variation of a basic curriculum contract activity package developed by a group of fourth- and fifth-grade teachers in the South Orangetown, New York public schools.

The contract combines the instructional objectives (written behaviorally) with a series of required activities through which the students may reinforce their learning and demonstrate their mastery. Additional media resource alternatives are to be identified by the pupils and will, in part, vary for each individual's contract. The teachers developed assignments and attached them to the contract. The reporting alternatives were built into the activity alternatives list and were not separated. The number of required activity alternatives varied with the students and were determined on the basis of student ability to work independently and effectively. Appropriate tests were used.

In the absence of an abundance of resource alternatives through which the students may learn the required information, it became necessary in this case for the teachers to supply the data. This was done through an introductory lecture and discussion with simultaneous taping of the lecture, which then became available to the students for reinforcement.

A Newspaper Study Curriculum Contract Activity Package (Combined Behavioral Objectives and Required Activity Alternatives)

1. Given different sections of a newspaper, you will correctly match each section to its correct definition with 100% accuracy. In addition, select any four of the following six activities to complete.
    (a) Bring in examples of each section of a newspaper and place them on a bulletin board that correctly indicates that section of the newspaper.

(b) Make a booklet by compiling examples of each part of a newspaper.

(c) Given an article, you will write a headline of five words or less describing the major aspects of the article.

(d) Given an historical event, you will write a headline describing it.

(e) Write your own advertisement, editorial and letter to the editor on whichever topic you select.

(f) Clip human-interest pictures from a newspaper and write a caption and story to accompany them.

2. Given a news article, you will list Who, What, When, Where, Why and How under the proper headings.

   In addition, select any three of the following five activities to complete.

   (a) Given an article, you will identify and circle those parts of it that answer the six basic news story questions (Who, What, When, Where, Why and How).

   (b) Write your own article after being given the six basic news story questions.

   (c) Find and bring in an article and then answer the questions on the attached Worksheet #1.

   (d) Write a short statement that answers the six basic questions and then write a telegram (which communicates the basic ideas) in no more than 10 words.

   (e) Write an article that answers the six basic questions about the historical event that matches the headline you wrote.

3. Given the four types of geographical news, you will list each headline under the proper heading—local, state, national or international. (See Worksheet #2.)

   In addition, complete item (a) and two of the remaining four activities.

   (a) Select one national personality and follow his present career by collecting and reading newspaper and magazine articles about him/her that appear during a one-month period. You will then synthesize the information you have accumulated and write a one- or two-page report describing the person's current life and activities as you understand them to be, based on the accounts you have collected. Discuss your conclusions with at least three classmates who each have developed a similar report on either the same or other personalities. Together you must draw at least six general conclusions about the lives and activities of famous people today.

   (b) Categorize the various articles mounted on our bulletin board as either local, state, national or international in scope.

   (c) With a colored pencil, underline the different types of news (local, state, national, international) that you find in a single

Worksheet #1

NAME _____

DATE _____

Read the Article: *Week of Worry*

Answer the important questions: When, Where, Why, What, Who and How.

1. What is the main topic of the article?

2. What two problems developed when the spacecraft neared the moon?

3. Where did the splash-down take place?

4. When did the splash-down take place?

5. How was the main spacecraft made to re-enter the atmosphere?

6. Who was studying the causes for Apollo 13's trouble?

7. Why did U.S. space officials call it "the most critical situation" in the history of our space program?

---

newspaper edition and write across the article which kind of news it represents.

(d) Given a newspaper, you will answer questions about the various items in the paper that refer to local, state, national or international coverage and be able to identify where in the newspaper each type of news is most likely to be found.

(e) Locate on the world map the origin of news articles in a single newspaper edition and join the articles to their origin with colored string (which designates if the article is local, state, national or international).

4. Given a list of newspaper terms, you will circle the three terms that most closely indicate the main purposes of a newspaper. (See Worksheet #3.)

Worksheet #2

NAME _____

DATE _____

Types of Geographical News

Directions: Put each headline under the proper heading.
LOCAL:

STATE:

NATIONAL:

INTERNATIONAL:

In addition, select any two of the following six activities:
   (a) Follow a stock in the financial section of the newspaper and chart its daily progress on a graph.
   (b) Write a book, movie, play or television review.
   (c) Write in words for those that are missing in a comic strip.
   (d) Cut out an advertisement and write your own slogan for it.
   (e) Write advertisements for things you want to sell.
   (f) Cut out advertisements, editorials and articles and demonstrate that they are fair, "slanted," opinionated or propaganda.
5. Given the definitions of 17 newspaper terms, you will relate at least 15 of them correctly. (See Worksheet #3.)
   In addition, complete three of the following five activities.
   (a) Make up a skit using the terms of the newspaper correctly.
   (b) Complete the crossword puzzle by filling in the spaces with the correct words that match the numbered definitions.
   (c) Complete the cryptogram and unjumble the letters to form words.

Worksheet #3

NAME _____

DATE _____

Purposes of the Newspaper

Directions: From the list of words below, circle the three main
purposes of a newspaper.

Dateline

Lead

Inform

National

Assignment

Copy

Cover

Entertain

Feature

Deadline

Byline

Copyright

Advise

Editorial

Sports

Finances

Classified Ads

(d) Orally define the terms of a newspaper to your teacher.

(e) Complete the fill-in-the-blank exercises of newspaper terms.

Each of these assignments may be completed individually, in pairs or in
small teams (three to six), as preferred by each student.

Worksheet #4

NAME_____

DATE_____

Parts of a Newspaper

Directions: Match the letter of the definition to the number of the word
           it correctly describes.

_____ 1. General News

_____ 2. Editorial

_____ 3. Society or Women's Page

_____ 4. Amusements

_____ 5. Sports

_____ 6. Financial and Business

_____ 7. Classified Advertisements

_____ 8. Comics

a. This section contains news about local, state, national and world sports events as well as people who are well known in sports.

b. This section contains world, national, state and local news. It is usually found in the front section of the newspaper.

c. This section contains comic strips, cartoons, puzzles and games.

d. This section contains articles that express the opinion of the editor or publisher of the newspaper.

e. This section contains news that will help businessmen and people who are interested in business.

f. This section contains news about fashions, clubs, social events and household hints.

g. This section lists information about radio, television, theater and movies.

h. This section contains Help Wanted ads, For Sale ads, Wanted to Buy ads and Real Estate ads. Sometimes the Lost and Found columns appear in this part too.

Media Resource Alternatives

Books

1. Ault, Phil. *News Around the Clock: Press Associations in Action.* New York: Dodd, Mead & Co., 1962. (Gray—traces the process of gathering the news to its actual appearance in the newspaper—talks about AP and UPI.)
2. Bartow, Edith Merwin. *News and These United States.* Funk & Wagnalls, 1952.
3. Baskette, Bastian, Case. *Editing the Day's News.* New York: The Macmillan Company, 1965. (Black.)
4. Berger, Meyer. *The Story of the New York Times.* New York: Simon and Schuster, Inc., 1951.
5. Bonner, M. G. *The Real Book About Journalism.* New York: Garden City Books, 1960. (Picture of newsman on cover—the story of the American newspaper—history and workings.)
6. Epstein, Sam and Beryl. *The First Book of News.* New York: Franklin Watts, Inc., 1965. (Red—traces the history of news—from the Greeks to the modern free press and the workings of a paper.)
7. Faber, Doris. *Behind the Headlines: The Story of Newspapers.* New York: Pantheon Books, 1963. (Black and white—dramatic account of how the editors, reporters and correspondents put out a daily newspaper.)
8. Hale, William Harlan. *Horace Greeley.* New York: Harper & Brothers, 1950.
9. Hohenberg, John, ed. *The Pulitzer Prize Story.* New York: Columbia University Press, 1959.
10. Jones, Robert W. *Journalism in the United States.* E. P. Dutton & Co., 1947.
11. Merrill, John C. *A Handbook of the Foreign Press.* Baton Rouge: Louisiana State University Press, 1959.
12. Meyer, Gerard Previn. *Pioneers of the Newspapers.* New York: Rand McNally & Co., 1961. (Blue, orange and white—the first newspapers in America.)
13. Morris, Richard B., and Louis L. Snyder, eds. *A Treasury of Great Reporting.* New York: Simon and Schuster, Inc. 1949.
14. Mott, Frank Luther. *American Journalism: A History of Newspapers in the U.S. Through 250 Years, 1690 to 1940,* The Macmillan Company, 1941.
15. *American Journalism, 1690-1960.* New York: The Macmillan Company, 1962.
16. Smith, Merriman. *Thank You, Mr. President.* New York: Harper & Brothers, 1946.

17. Sootin, Laura. *Let's Go to a Newspaper.* New York: G. P. Putnam's Sons, 1956. (Black, white and green.)
18. Tebbel, John. *The Life and Good Times of William Randolph Hearst.* New York: E. P. Dutton & Co., Inc., 1952.

Films
  My Life as a Reporter
  Developing a Class Newspaper
Tapes
  (Teacher-developed) Introductory Lecture on Newspaper Writing
  (Student-developed) Responses to Worksheets #1 through #4
Dittos
  The Parts of a Newspaper
  Geographical Coverage of the News
Materials
  Bulletin board exhibits
  Student-developed books and completed and corrected assignments
Film Loop
  Analyzing a news story (Who, What, When, Where, How and Why)
Newspapers
  Current editions to be supplied by the students
Picture Files

  Various pictures can be obtained from various magazines, and picture files are obtainable from libraries

Contract Activity Alternatives

Select and complete at least *four** of the following seven activities.

1. Divide a bulletin board into sections and place news clippings under each appropriate heading:

   Local News   National News
   State News   International News

Be responsible for keeping the board current, attractive and well-organized.
2. Mount a newspaper story on the bulletin board. Draw lines to the Who, What, When, Why, Where and How of the item. Ask a classmate to check your additions to the bulletin board. The classmate should initial the article when he agrees that you lined it correctly.
3. Set up a gallery of photos of prominent people in the world. Post them around the room so that students can begin to relate names and faces in the news.

---

*The number of activities assigned depends on the teacher's appraisal of the ability, maturity and interest of the student.

Write a story about one person.
Follow that person in the news.
Discuss your story with at least three classmates and draw conclusions about the lives and activities of famous people today.

4. Using a map of the world, display news items with strings pointing out the areas where the story occurred. Have at least two other classmates check the accuracy of your display. They may initial the display when they agree that it is correct.

5. Story writing:

Clip human-interest pictures and remove the original captions.
Ask two other students to write captions for the pictures.
Ask two other students to write original stories for the pictures.
Compare the results of their captions and stories.

6. Make a bulletin board displaying advertisements cut from magazines. Choose one and write a slogan of not more than 15 words to make your friend want to buy it.

7. Put a comic strip on the bulletin board with the words in the balloons missing, and then write your own words. Read your comic strip to at least two other children. Ask for their reactions to your work.

TESTS

CONTRACT TEST RECORD   NAME_____

DATE_____

Circle the appropriate use of this test.

(1) *DIAGNOSTIC TEST*   (2) *SELF-TEST*   (3) *TERMINAL TEST*

Score obtained:___   Score obtained:___   Score obtained:___

Degree of proficiency
required:___

MASTERY STILL REQUIRED IN INSTRUCTIONAL OBJECTIVES:

(1)_____ (2)_____ (3)_____

_____   _____

_____   _____

_____

_____

SAMPLE CONTRACT TEST QUESTIONS (INFORMATION)

1.   Abbreviation of Associated Press.

    a. Dateline   c. Byline
    b. UPI   d. AP

2.   A story that a reporter has been asked to cover.
    a. Assignment   c. Feature
    b. Dateline   d. Cover

3.   A headline in large letters running across the entire width of the page.

    a. Lead   c. Wirephoto
    b. Banner   d. Copyright

4.   Reporter's regular routine for covering news sources.

    a. Dummy   c. Beat
    b. Cover   d. Proofreader

5.   Signature of a writer appearing at the head of a story.

    a. Copyright   c. UPI
    b. Byline   d. Kill

6.   All material for publication, whether written stories, pictures or advertising.

    a. Copy   c. Deadline
    b. Feature   d. Banner

7.   An author's exclusive rights of property in his work for a certain period of time.

    a. Copyright   c. Lead
    b. AP   d. Dummy

8.   To get all the facts for a news report, a reporter must＿＿＿＿the event.

    a. Proofread   c. Cover
    b. Wirephoto   d. Feature

9.   The lines at the beginning of a story giving the place and sometimes the date of the reported incident.

    a. Dateline   c. Byline
    b. Deadline   d. Lead

10.   Time by which all copy for an edition must be completed.

    a. UPI   c. Deadline
    b. AP   d. Copyright

11.   A diagram or layout of a newspaper page, showing the placement of stories, headlines, pictures and advertisements.

    a. Copy   c. Lead
    b. Dummy   d. Dateline

12. A story in which interest lies in some factor other than the news value. Usually written to entertain, it might be a story of a lost boy's experiences or a columnist's feelings about Paris.

    a. Deadline   c. Cover
    b. Feature   d. Banner

13. To strike out copy or take out type not to be printed.

    a. Kill   c. Byline
    b. Proofread   d. Beat

14. The first few sentences or the first paragraph of a news story, containing the summary or the introduction to the story. It follows the general rule of telling Who, What, When, Where, Why and How.

    a. Byline   c. Dateline
    b. Proofread   d. Lead

15. One who reads proof and marks errors.

    a. Proofreader   c. Wirephoto
    b. UPI   d. Dummy

16. Abbreviation for United Press International.

    a. Cover   c. UPI
    b. Beat   d. Deadline

17. An Associated Press machine that both receives and sends pictures by wire.

    a. Banner   c. Beat
    b. Wirephoto   d. Dummy

Independent Contracts

"Independent contracts" are outlines of study specifically developed for individual children who would function better or more efficiently in a totally different curriculum area than is prescribed for most children in the class. These are not curriculum contracts, for they represent highly individualized planning and concentration for children who deviate from the majority of youngsters in their given group situation. These independent contracts vary from the structured outline of development because of the special needs of the students and the teachers' diagnoses and prescriptions.

An Independent Contract for a Child
Who Does Not Like to Read or Write

You will note that in this sample the resource, activity and reporting alternatives that relate to each behavioral objective directly follow the objective and are incorporated into one item under "Activity."

Background

Joey is the six-and-one-half-year-old son of a TV producer and the youngest of four children. He belongs to a busy, active household, with everyone, including his mother, coming and going to activities in accordance with their interests.

Joey is considered quite bright, makes friends easily, has an active imagination and is fairly independent. His reading progress has been slow but steady. He loves to bring interesting objects to school and report to his classmates. His special interests are anything "scientific" and collecting shells, rocks and leaves. His idea of a treat is to watch a TV special on the subject of whales, sharks or dolphins. His favorite place is the aquarium.

Joey is in first grade. His teacher describes the class as being on an "individualized learning program." The reading medium is i.t.a. On occasion, Joey disturbs the class by getting up and marching around the room noisily. His teacher says that much of the time Joey refuses to copy an experience chart or work an assignment in a workbook. He usually just sits quietly. It has been discovered recently that he has taught himself to tell time by observing the classroom clock, manipulating a "learning clock" in the classroom and asking questions at home.

Contract Considerations

1. A conference with Joey's parents is planned to outline the proposal for independent study in the area of his greatest interest, science.
2. It must be pointed out also that apparently Joey's difficulties with writing (a small-muscle act) may be seen as physical immaturity. This correlates with his reluctance to tie his shoelaces (an agonizing task for him) and his lack of interest in playing "catch." He enjoys large-motor-muscle activities like bike riding, roller skating and fishing.
3. The active cooperation of his parents will be enlisted to provide encouragement and praise for Joey's efforts, to take him on frequent trips and to assist with his projects.
4. Activities will be developed with a view toward a minimum of reading and writing. The use of oral reports and media will be encouraged.
5. It will be pointed out that an intended goal is to help Joey develop interest and skill in writing. As his skill increases, it is hoped that he will attempt writing more frequently.

A Science Contract for Joey (85% Accuracy Will Be Required in Each Category)

1. *Behavioral Objective:* Look at a set of 20 pictures and be able to separate them into piles of "animal" pictures, "vegetable" pictures and "mineral" pictures.

   Activity: (a) Look at *The True Science Library* by Illa Podendorf (The True Book Series), Children's Press, Chicago, 1963, Vols. 1-8. (b) Look at *The Golden Book Encyclopedia of Natural Science,* The Golden Press, 1957. *Test:* Separate 20 pictures into three piles labeled "animal," "vegetable" or "mineral."

2. *Behavioral Objective:* Tell about the foods eaten by at least three animals.

   Activity: (a) Visit one or more of the following places: a zoo, an aquarium, a kennel, a farm, a museum. (b) Give an oral report.

3. *Behavioral Objective:* Collect sea shells and be able to identify correctly five types usually found in our area.

   Activity: (a) Visit the seashore. (b) Look at *Houses from the Sea* by Alice E. Gondey, Scribner's, 1959; or *First Book of Sea Shells* by Betty Cavanna, Watts, 1955. (c) Make labels for the shells.

4. *Behavioral Objective:* Be able to describe three things that are important to the health of goldfish.

   Activity: (a) Look at *Twenty Little Fishes* by Else Bostelman. (b) Care for the goldfish aquarium in the classroom. (c) Report on the care of fishes.

5. *Behavioral Objective:* Be able to tell an interesting story about why you like a certain animal best and include three facts about that creature.

   Activity: (a) Dictate the story into the tape recorder. (b) Make a papier-mâché model of the animal selected. (c) Paint a picture of the place where this animal lives.

6. *Behavioral Objective:* Be able to complete accurately the following sentence, "The best way to care for a turtle is . . ."

   Activity: (a) Look at the *World Book Encyclopedia.* (b) Complete the sentence on a typewriter.

7. *Behavioral Objective:* Selecting the letters from a box, be able to place on the flannel board the names of five fish in 20 minutes.

   Activity: (a) Visit the aquarium. (b) Visit the Museum of Natural History. (c) Look at *Fishes* by Herbert S. Zim, Golden Press.

8. *Behavioral Objective:* Write the names of five types of sharks on cards and match the names with the pictures of the sharks.

   Activity: (a) Visit the aquarium. (b) Visit the Museum of Natural History. (c) Look at *Sharks,* Herbert S. Zim, Morrow.

9. *Behavioral Objective:* Correctly make up at least one sentence about a new season.

   Activity: (a) Draw a picture to illustrate the season. (b) Select appropriate words written on cards. (c) Place the cards under the picture in a sentence that describes the scene you drew. (d) Find the beginning and end of the season on a calendar.

10. *Behavioral Objective:* Draw a series of pictures showing the development of a plant from a seed.

    Activity: (a) Make a shoebox movie theater. (b) Make a scrapbook. (c) Grow a plant from seed. (d) Look at *Flowers,* Herbert S. Zim, Golden Press.

11. *Behavioral Objective:* Tell and show your classmates three things that are the same and three things that are different about three or more kinds of leaves.

    Activity: (a) Give a report while showing leaves on an opaque projector. (b) Look at leaves through a microscope.

12. *Behavioral Objective:* Make up a story about a dolphin, and include at least one way in which the dolphin is unusual.

    Activity: (a) Visit the aquarium. (b) Look at *Dolphins* by Patricia Lauber, Random House, 1963. (c) Type the story.

13. *Behavioral Objective:* Participate in a school-sponsored science fair by entering your collection of rocks that are labeled and identified. Include at least five types usually found in this region.

    Activity: (a) Look at one of the following: *My Hobby Is Collecting Rocks and Minerals* by David E. Jansen, 1955; *Adventure Book of Rocks,* Eva Knox Evans, Capital, 1955; *Rocks All Around Us* by Anne Terry White, Random House, 1959. (b) Visit different topographical regions to collect rocks. (c) Build your own display case.

14. *Behavioral Objective:* Be able to demonstrate and use a weather instrument and keep a daily chart for one week.

    Activity: (a) Look at *I Like Weather,* Aileen Lucia Fisher, Crowell, 1963. (b) You and your parents will build at least two weather instruments at home. (c) Keep a daily record of the temperature during one season. (d) Visit the Weather Bureau. (e) Report to the class.

15. *Behavioral Objective:* Be able to report on the progress of tadpoles collected from a stream.

    Activity: (a) Look at *Golden Book Encyclopedia.* (b) Draw a picture of each change of development. (c) Write a daily log of a tadpole's growth. (d) Discuss the progress of tadpoles with at least three of your classmates and your teacher. Tape the discussion so that other classmates may hear it later.

16. *Behavioral Objective:* Make a landscape showing at least five topographical features and label at least three features correctly.

    Activity: (a) You can make a landscape using one or more of the following materials: clay, dirt, sand, plaster of paris, pebbles. Display it. (b) Visit a mountain top and a valley and discuss what you see with at least two classmates.

17. *Behavioral Objective:* Be able to measure, with a ruler, five marked distances in 10 minutes.
    Activity: (a) Record the distance a pet turtle can walk in 5 minutes. (b) See if your friends can guess the answer correctly. (c) Does the distance change at different times?

18. *Behavioral Objective:* Given a vocabulary list of 10 words, use each of the words correctly in a sentence.
    Activity: (a) Dictate a sentence for each word into the tape recorder. (b) Type a sentence for each word.

19. *Behavioral Objective:* Be able to use a teacher-made annual bar graph.
    Activity: (a) Write the names of your classmates on small squares and paste them onto a graph according to the month in which their birthdays fall. Ask your classmates to check your graph to see that their names have been placed in the correct square.

(Prepared by Dulcie A. Freeman, Long Beach, New York)

Testing

For this contract, because of Joey's difficulty in writing, the teacher chose to pretest him verbally. His parents used the initial pretest as a self-test for Joey (again, verbally), and the teacher asked Joey to complete the terminal test (which was identical to the initial pretest and self-test) in writing. Joey did so with 100% accuracy.

Advice to the Teacher:
Student Interaction and Record Keeping

It is desirable for students to learn at their own rate and pace, select resource materials based on their personal perception of their own strengths and weaknesses and have many opportunities to exercise choice in the learning process. It is not desirable, however, for students to continuously work independently without benefit of peer-group or other interaction in the learning process.

Part of each student's school day should include peer-centered discussions, cooperative project ventures, small-group reporting (students should rarely address an entire class), the sharing of information and personal perceptions, challenged analysis and group decision making (Photo 4-1). Unless these experiences are provided for students, home-conceived biases and restrictive learning methods will

Photo 4-1. *Part of each student's day should include the sharing of information with others. Peer and multiage interactions reinforce learning. (Photograph courtesy of Freeport Public Schools, Freeport, New York.)*

continue to dominate the manner in which pupils think through problems, attack issues and form conclusions. Exposure to different learning and thinking styles may help many youngsters mature rapidly and vary their approaches to the acquisitions of concepts and knowledge.

A variety of group-centered teaching techniques like team learning, circles of knowledge, simulations and role playing should be built into every contract developed by the teacher and made an integral part of every student's learning procedure (see Part III).

Individualized instruction through the use of contracts makes lesson planning obsolete for the modern teacher. If contracts are employed, every child will be working independently on varying phases of his own plan while selecting media resource alternatives that most appeal to him, determining which activity and reporting alternatives he will use and increasing or decreasing his pace and rate of growth according to his mood, ability to concentrate, motivation and self-discipline. It is obvious that an individual teacher could not keep an accurate accounting of what is being learned on a given day (or during a given period), by whom, with which resources or at what speed, by formulating a traditional lesson plan for the class. In addition, typical lesson plans have little value or place in a contract-centered learning environment, and a suitable substitute must be devised so that the teacher may keep a record of each student's progress and growth.

Teachers will find that a 12" x 14" accordion folder labeled with the pupil's name will serve as an adequate storage file. It should hold the youngster's initial diagnostic test or appraisal, contract, completed worksheets and assignments, self-test and terminal test. In addition, if suitable in size and weight, developed materials such as tapes, projects, original compositions and similar products should be included. At the completion of each contract topic, the teacher should add a grade to the contract folder and send the entire packet home for parental inspection. This folder, in addition to the teacher's regular record-keeping system (grade book, achievement lists, report cards), should represent a step forward in recording pupil progress. Assessment in this procedure aids in diagnosing progress and prescribing contracts and learning experiences.

Individual pupil diagnosis, prescription and evaluation that aid in continuing teacher- and self-diagnosis for the student are central to the contract and individualizing process. Minicase studies and appraisals by the teacher will aid all concerned in the current and future education and self-actualization of each child.

III

Using Effective
Teaching Strategies

5

Team Learning and Circles of Knowledge: Using Group Process Techniques to Divide and Conquer Instructional Problems

Why Teaming Works!
The Need for Socialization and Group Learning

A good program of individualized instruction permits students to work together in pairs and teams as well as alone (Photos 5-1, 5-2, 5-3). Building small-group interactions into the learning process prevents youngsters from becoming isolated and lonely. By working together, students spark each other's ideas, help each other to learn, exchange points of view and share the responsibility for learning, so that self-reliance does not become too burdensome. In addition to these advantages, learning together in teams is fun, and contributions toward a cooperative effort can earn a member of a group recognition, respect and affection.[1] Indeed, confidence as an individual can be enhanced through success in the group.

Finally, a well-designed group technique will provide the "frequency, intensity and variety" that insures effective learning and eliminates boredom.

---

[1] Bernard M. Bass, *Organization Psychology* (Boston, Mass.: Allyn & Bacon, Inc., 1965), p. 13.

Photos 5-1, 5-2, 5-3. *A good program of individualized instruction permits students to work together in pairs and in teams as well as alone. (Photographs 5-1 and 5-2 courtesy of Freeport Public Schools, Freeport, New York; Photograph 5-3 courtesy of West Hartford Public Schools, West Hartford, Connecticut—Robert L. May, photographer.)*

Photos 5-1, 5-2, 5-3 (Contd.)

Managing a Heterogeneous Class to
Provide for Individual Differences

After a student clearly understands his objectives and how they may be mastered, he should be free to begin achieving them in whichever way he decides. Some students will begin by working independently; others will choose to work closely with a classmate or chum; still others will form task forces or committees of three to six.

Available media will almost always be in constant use. Learning stations, interest centers, game tables and library resources will be occupied by students intent on obtaining specific information.

Art corners and "little theater" areas will be the center of creativity, while students, individually or in groups, will lounge on carpeted sections of the room or study in comfort on available couches or armchairs. Few children will elect to remain uninvolved, and, if some do, the teacher can work directly with them until they become secure in this new type of learning environment.

Charts indicating students who are available to assist others with the use of equipment or software should be posted in an appropriate area. Supplies should be easily accessible, but students must assume the responsibility for organizing and keeping them in good condition.

The teacher will plan her time so that she can work directly with each of the small groups of students and all of those working individually. She will ask pointed questions related to the objectives of the children she is questioning. She will ask what they are working on, how far they have come, what they are having difficulty with and how much they understand about what they say they have been studying. As she detects weaknesses and special areas of difficulty among students, she will cluster small groups (three to eight) around her in a section of the room and teach them what they should know. The smallness of the cluster groups will permit her to get to know each child well and will make her aware of any emerging or potential problems. Individual conferences with the ·teacher either should be scheduled by arrangement or spontaneous, as the need arises, but they should occur at least every other day. In between, the teacher will supervise the studying and interaction of the children by sitting with them, stopping for a few moments to chat, checking assignments, questioning information and overseeing the small-group interactions that should be built into each child's program.

How Teaming Frees the Teacher to Facilitate Learning

While students are working together in teams, the teacher is free to observe each of the functioning groups and see how individual children relate to each other and to their group as a whole. The view of a student in relation to his peers is an important one and frequently provides the teacher with insights into the child that she might not obtain under other conditions.

As teams are engaged in completing group tasks, the teacher may work in depth with either individuals or small numbers of students. Fewer children are likely to require instant attention once they have been trained to turn to and rely on their team members to lend assistance and guidance. For the few youngsters who "need" her, the teacher may institute a system whereby any student may write his/her name on the chalkboard (or a chart) under the label "I Need You." The understanding must be that they may not ever interrupt the teacher while she is working with a child or group. The students may expect that as soon as the teacher finishes her present task, she will look at the board to learn who requires her attention and seek them out to render assistance before she begins to work with the next group.

Team Learning: Simple and Complex Techniques

Team learning is an excellent technique for introducing new material to children. Begin by writing one or more short paragraphs that include whatever you want the students to learn. Beginning readers may be able to absorb between three and six sentences collectively; able 12-year-olds could probably digest 20 to 25 sentences divided into four or five paragraphs.

At the end of the written materials, list a series of questions that should be answered by the group. Some of the questions may be directly related to the written material; for these, students may refer back to the paragraphs and identify the correct information. Some of the questions should *not* be answerable through the written content. For these it will be necessary for the group members to discuss the possible alternative answers before selecting the one(s) they wish to use.

When the written materials are ready, the students may divide themselves into groups of between five and eight. (If teachers prefer, they may assign students to a group.) The teams may be either homogeneous or heterogeneous in character, for either arrangement works well.

Once the groups are seated in a closely knit, round circle on chairs, hassocks or the floor, if carpeted (desks are unnecessary and undesirable for this technique), tell the team(s) that each group must have a "recorder." It does not matter how the group acquires its recorder; it may elect, appoint, accept a volunteer or draft someone for the position. Only one person in the group (the recorder) needs to write the group's responses to the questions. Make this point clear and add that spelling and grammar are not the target for this exercise; indeed, short, succinct phrases to indicate the group's responses are all that are essential. [Teachers will find that many team members will write the responses, even though they have been told that it is unnecessary for anyone other than the recorder to do so. When this occurs, overlook it, for some children (and adults) need to write the answers to learn them.]

Tell the students that anyone in a team may help another member of that team but no one may help *another* team. Ask them how they can keep from helping other teams. Let them realize that to avoid giving away answers it will be necessary for each team to confer quietly. Tell them that if another team hears their answers to a question it may use those answers; to protect themselves (and their answers), they will have to work quietly within their groups.

After forming the teams, giving the directions and distributing the materials, the teacher may walk slowly among the groups to study the process of team learning. Initially the children will begin to read along, trying to absorb the information and concepts by themselves. As they continue into the subject matter, one or two children will begin to ask their teammates specific words or the meanings of words. Gradually conversation will begin and the discussion will lead to clarification of meanings and the development of responses to the questions that follow the paragraphed materials. Occasionally, children will begin to laugh or argue; here and there directions will be accepted or rejected; enthusiasm will build and the group will begin to achieve camaraderie.

After a suitable interval (this will vary with the children and their ability to function in groups), the teacher should indicate that the teams have "only 2 more minutes to complete their work." If this were an arbitrary time limit imposed on individuals it would be oppressive, but members of a team tend to identify with their group and only partial completion of an assignment is not an intimidating factor, when it is shared among many. The teacher will have to be sensitive to group progress, but when two-thirds of the groups have completed their team learning assignments it would be wise to call a halt to the activity.

An alternate method would be to permit each group to complete its assignment at its leisure. When a group has finished, one of its members may notify the teacher, who could then work with the single group as a whole. If the teacher is busy with one group, a competent student, who has experienced the technique and is certain of the correct answers, may be assigned to work with another team until the teacher is no longer occupied.

When the teacher wants to work directly with all the groups, she will halt the group discussions at the point where she believes most of the children are ready or near-ready to discuss their teams' responses. The teacher will ask that discussion end and that the recorders all monitor their individual group's answers carefully. The teacher should call on one child to read the first question. She will then ask a recorder from another group to supply the answers to that question. Each of the teams' recorders will be cautioned to listen to the response offered by the speaker and, if their group had a similar answer, to cross that answer off their list so that the answers are gradually marked off each group's list. In this way, after several children have responded, only those answers that have not yet been spoken will remain on each list.

One by one, each of the questions will be read by a different student, and various members of each team will have opportunities to give their group's answers to the questions (always crossing off the answer that is called out). If a team member is called upon for an answer, the recorder may quickly pass the answer sheet to him because the answers are group responses and belong to each member. Eventually, the teacher and class will proceed through all of the questions, permitting most of the team members to participate in the responding. In this way, no errors or misinformation will be retained, all questions will be answered and everyone will have had a chance to participate. Members of teams that may not have completed all the written answers to the questions may respond verbally as the questions are read. For additional interest and stimulation, a teacher may assign a number to each team, place the numeral representing the team on the chalkboard and award points for each correct or creative answer. This method causes competition among the teams but the rivalry is friendly, for children do not mind "losing" as a member of a team as acutely as they do as an individual.

Another form of team learning requires more active participation by the teacher. Initially the process begins in the same way: the teams are formed, the directions are given and the materials are distributed. The teacher then invites one group at a time to a given area of the classroom, where she presents the information or concepts to be studied in pictorial or graphic form on a transparency, picture or slide. Grouping the team members around the projector (overhead, opaque or slide) in a semicircle, she then describes the information dramatically, making every attempt to involve the students in the discussion. Because she is so physically close to the team members, she will be able to tell whether each student understands the concept or fact, where areas of difficulty might develop or whether students want specific questions answered. During the short period (5 to 8 minutes) in which she keeps the group with her, she actually reinforces the information that appears in the distributed materials, but does so in an interesting way.

Each group, in turn, comes to the teacher's area and participates in the discussion-lecture about the information. It is wise to restrict the number of groups to a maximum of four. If the teacher tires of repetition, she may appoint a bright student to listen to the first two minilectures and discussions and then conduct the third, and possibly, the fourth. The opportunity to teach peers is a good one for the student who does the teaching and is stimulating and motivating for the ones being taught.

After all of the teams have worked with the teacher (or the student assistant) and returned to their seats, the teacher will circulate around the area listening to the students' discussions to determine specific difficulties or identify misunderstandings. When most of the teams have completed their assignments, the teacher may lead the class as a whole through the reading of the questions and team answers as described in the first part of this section.

This slightly more sophisticated form of team learning enables the teacher to present the information to the children verbally and dramatically as well as visually.

Analyzing the Process

Team learning provides students with the concepts and facts

that they should learn visually (printed matter and/or transparencies, pictures or slides), through listening (the teacher presentation and the peer-group and teacher-class discussions) and sometimes through touch or physical action (writing, crossing off, illustrating). Students read the information, discuss it among the team members, write or dictate answers, read the answers, discuss the answers with the teacher and the larger group and reach conclusions. This method provides active student participation in a learning process that removes time, distance and other barriers to learning. Students can relate to each other in a circle of chairs without desks, thus improving cohesiveness, group morale, communication and achievement.

Sample Team Learning Lessons

Team learning may be used to introduce and teach material in every curriculum area. The following example demonstrates how social studies materials may be used in this group process.

The Sociology of India (Suggested Grade Levels 4-6): The Joint Family System

Objective: Be able to explain at least five ways that the joint family system in India differs from our family system in the United States.

Date_____

Team Members

1._____   5._____

2._____   6._____

3._____   7._____

4._____   8._____

Recorder_____

In India, a family includes the father, the mother and the children. When the family is poor, both parents work. Sometimes, even when the family is rich, both parents work.

In a poor Indian family the wife does all the housework and cooking, in addition to her work outside the home. She gets up at 5 a.m. or earlier to do so. As a rule men do not help with housework, but the children do.

At a very early age, children in India begin to act as baby sitters for younger brothers and sisters or for other infants within the *joint* family. They carry the younger ones on their hips wherever they go during the time parents are away. Children also help the family by taking care of the cattle and doing odd jobs.

A son is very important to the family. When he is old enough to marry, his wife will bring a gift of money, called a *dowry*, which helps to stabilize the family economy. A daughter, however, takes away money as dowry when she marries.

The son also is important because he takes part in the funeral ceremony for his father. All children, both boys and girls, are very much loved in India. A childless family is pitied.

Grandparents, if alive, are very much a part of the joint family; in fact, they rule the household. The grandmother has more to say in decision making than the mother, and the men in the house have more privileges than women. The grandfather as the family's "elder" has to be respected for his age, experience and wisdom, even when he is not able to contribute to the family's support.

If the grandparents have other sons, they too have the right to stay in the household or build houses of their own on the family property. All the sons are expected to help support the family, but if they are too young to work or unable to find employment, it is the duty of the other members of the family, particularly the older brother, to support them.

When the sons get married, they are entitled to raise their families as part of the joint family, sharing the same house and the family's food. The wife of a younger brother has the least voice in family matters, but she has her full share of responsibilities. She must follow the orders of women in the house who are senior to her; in return, she and her children have the right to full protection and care as long as her husband lives.

Assignment:

1. If you were an Indian father, would you want to have many sons?_____

    Yes or No

    Give three reasons for your answer:

    A._____

    B._____

    C._____

2. Give three reasons why someone might prefer being a grandparent in India rather than a grandparent in the United States.

    A._____

    B._____

    C._____

3. Give three reasons why someone might prefer being a grandparent in the United States rather than a grandparent in India.

    A._____

    B._____

    C._____

4. Why do you think "... age, experience and wisdom ..." are respected in India?

    _____

    _____

5. Give three qualities that are respected in the United States.

    A._____

    B._____

C._____

6. Give three reasons why a young married woman might prefer to live in India rather than in the United States.

   A._____

   B._____

   C._____

7. Give three reasons why a young married woman might prefer to live in the United States rather than in India.

   A._____

   B._____

   C._____

8. A. Does India favor youth or age?_____

   Explain:_____

   _____

   _____

   _____

   _____

   B. Does the United States favor youth or age?_____

   Explain:_____

   _____

   _____

   _____

9. What is good about the Indian joint family system?

   A._____

   B._____

   C._____

10. What is good about the family system in the United States?

A._____

B._____

C._____

[Some of the content material was abstracted from the Teacher's Guide for "India," *Discover Your World* Series (New York: AEVAC, Inc., 1969), pp. 7-10.]

An interdisciplinary approach to learning may be easily accomplished by combining language arts (poetry, literature, drama, plays) or music with an appropriate social studies topic. The following team learning exercise blends several skills (including creative drawing and writing) with social studies.

History Through Poetry (Suggested Grade Levels 3-7): Abraham Lincoln

Objective: Be able to explain some of the things in Abraham Lincoln's life that may have influenced him.

... Lincoln owed nothing to his birth, everything to his growth ... he grew and strengthened in the real stuff of dignity and greatness.[2]

Team Members	*Date*
1. ———————	4. ———————
2. ———————	5. ———————
3. ———————	6. ———————

Recorder _____

Young Abe Lincoln[3]

He had so little at his birth—
A one-room cabin, none too tight,
With walls of logs and floor of earth,
One door, one pane to let in light;
The very least of bed and board
A frontier cabin could afford.

He had so little growing up
When splitting fence-rails was the rule.
His chances filled a spoon, not cup:
A few uncertain months at school,
A book or two, and little more.
Yet Abe had dreams worth waiting for.

---

[2] Dorothy Carrico Wood (ed.), *This Nation* (Cleveland : The World Publishing Company, 1967), p. 74.

[3] *Ibid.,* p. 75.

He had so little all those years
When getting-on seems uppermost—
He had no means, no friendly peers,
No family tree of which to boast.
And yet . . . wherever was a lad
Who went so far on what he had!

by Aileen Fisher and Olive Rabe

Assignment: (Groups need not be given identical assignments. The teacher will assign the numbered tasks as they are appropriate to the children in each group.)

1. What are some of the phrases in the poem that tell you that Abraham Lincoln's family was very poor?

   A._____

   B._____

   C._____

   D._____

   E._____

2. Which phrase tells you that he had no friends of his own age?

   _____

3. Why do you think he had "no friendly peers"?

   _____

   _____

4. Which phrase hints at what helped Abe overcome being poor and alone?

   _____

   _____

5. Write a short group poem explaining what Abe Lincoln had to overcome to become one of the greatest Presidents we have ever had.

   _____

_____

_____

_____

_____

6. *Draw* the inside of the one-room log cabin described in the poem.

7. What is meant by a "family tree"?

_____

_____

_____

8. What is meant by a cabin which is "... none too tight"?

_____

_____

_____

A "detriment" is something that works against you. Being poor can be a detriment, for it is more difficult to get food, fuel for warmth or an education when you do not have the money. Being *alone* can be a detriment, for it is more difficult to have courage or determination when there is no one to protect or love you.

9. Do you know the names of any other people who became famous or successful in spite of the detriments they had?

A._____

B._____

C._____

10. If you would like to read more about Abraham Lincoln, you can get any of the following books:

Genevieve Foster, *Abraham Lincoln's World* (New York: Charles Scribner's Sons, 1944). This is an informal, graphic

and different approach to what was going on in the world
during the lifetime of Abraham Lincoln.

Kenneth S. Giniger (ed.), *America, America, America* (New
York: Franklin Watts, Inc., 1957), pp. 94, 98, 101.

Louis Untermeyer (ed.), *The Golden Book of Quotations*
(New York: Golden Press, 1964), pp. 72-73.

Dorothy Carrico Wood (ed.), *This Nation* (Cleveland: The
World Publishing Company, 1967), pp. 52, 54, 62, 71, 75-82.

Even very young children respond favorably to poetry through
team learning. Try reproducing a simple poem that lends itself to
graphic representations[4] and build into the exercise many interesting
activities appropriate to the level of the children who will be working
with it. Team learning involves the students in cooperative instructional discussions in a pleasant, nonthreatening way and automatic-
ally provides the frequency, intensity and variety that helps children
retain and use information.

How to Organize and Group Circles of Knowledge

No small-group instructional technique rivals a "circle of knowledge" as a reinforcement process. This teaching strategy permits
students to:

1. Review previously learned information in an interesting way.
2. Focus their thinking on one major concept at a time.
3. Contribute to a group effort as part of a team.
4. Serve as catalysts for additional responses.
5. Develop ingenuity in helping team members to contribute.
6. Be exposed to and learn information without becoming bored.

Direct groups of between five and eight students to disperse
evenly about the room (area, center) and form several small circles.
Each group must have a recorder; again, the recorder may volunteer,
be elected, be appointed by the group members or "take a turn."
The teacher will either distribute a written question or problem
which has *multiple* possible answers to the group or write one on a
chalkboard or chart for all to see.

Each circle of knowledge will respond to the same question

---

[4] "Eletelephony," Laura E. Richards, *Read Me a Poem* (New York: Grosset and
Dunlap, 1964) p. 24; "The Little Turtle," Vachel Lindsay, *Time for Poetry* (Glenview,
Illinois: Scott, Foresman and Company, 1968), pp. 250-251 or "The Monkey and the
Crocodile," *ibid.*, p. 126.

simultaneously (but quietly). A member in each group is designated as the first to begin, and the answers are then provided by one member at a time in clockwise (or counterclockwise) fashion. No member may skip his turn and no one may provide an answer until the person directly before him has delivered his; therefore, the answers stop while a member is "thinking" or groping for a possible response. No teammate may "give" an answer to another, but the group may "act out" or pantomime "hints" to help the person remember an item, an answer or a possible response.

Photo 5-4. *The recorder writes the responses of each participant as the circle of knowledge continues. (Photograph courtesy of Freeport Public Schools, Freeport, New York.)*

Only the recorder may write, and he jots down (in a phrase or two only) the suggestions (answers, responses, thoughts) of each participant as the circle of knowledge continues (Photo 5-4).

At the end of a predetermined amount of time, the teacher calls a halt to the "knowledge" sharing and all recorders must stop writing the groups' answers. The *number* of responses conjured up by each group is noted, but credit is not given for quantity alone.

The teacher then repeats the question that was posed to the entire group. In turn, a representative from each circle offers one of the answers suggested by that group. When an answer is provided, every recorder in the room looks at the list of answers developed by his/her group. If that answer is on his circle's list, he crosses it off, thus gradually decreasing the length of the list until only the answers that have not yet been reported to the group remain. This procedure continues until no circle has any remaining answers on its list.

The answers given by each circle of knowledge can be awarded points that are then recorded on the board to produce competition among the teams. The teacher might decide that each correct response will earn 10 points and that the circle achieving the most points will be the winner. Any time an answer is challenged by a rival circle, the teacher must decide whether it is right or wrong. If the answer is right and the challenger incorrect, the challenger's circle loses 5 points. If the answer is incorrect and the challenger was right, the circle who sponsored the answer loses 10 points and the challenger's circle gains 5 points.

The review provided by the intergroup discussion, the responses and the challengers make a "circle of knowledge" an effective technique for reinforcement through student participation.

Horizontal and Vertical Discipline Clusters

Circles of knowledge may be formed around either horizontal (a topic question that requires information of several subjects) or vertical (a topic question relating to only one subject) discipline clusters. The following list indicates examples of both types:

Horizontal Discipline Clusters

- List the Ways That a Desert Child's Life Differs from Yours.

- List the Possible Causes of War.

- Why Hasn't a Woman Been Elected President of the United States?

- What Are Some Ways We Can Show People That We Like Them?

Vertical Discipline Clusters

- List as Many Adverbs as You Can.

- What Are the Economic Implications of the Caste System in India?

- What Are the Jobs a Fireman Must Do?

- What Are Some Rules We Should Follow When Our Class Takes a Trip?

Notice that to answer the horizontal discipline cluster questions, it would be necessary to demonstrate knowledge in several related subjects, such as history, economics, sociology, anthropology, geography or political science. In the vertical cluster, a knowledge of essentially one subject is required.

Charting New Activities and Variations:
The Roles of the Teacher, Aide, Student and Teacher Candidate

The grouping of pupils should be varied so that students have opportunities to work at several academic levels with youngsters of varying abilities. It is also advantageous to permit interage groupings when youngsters show similar interests or talents, or when both older and younger students can gain from joint group activities.

Many communities are planning intergenerational instructional activities to provide youngsters, their parents and their grandparents with opportunities to learn and work together, on the theory that understanding among the three groups will develop and expand with common experiences. Neighborhood centers are becoming the focus of adult education and after-school interests and, simultaneously, community parents and representatives are being trained to assist in the schools at the same time that junior and senior high school students are learning to work with elementary school pupils. New patterns of interage and intergenerational cooperation make possible many variations of grouping activities and enhanced learning.

Team Activities and Roles of Different Teaching Personnel

Activities	Variations	Personnel Functions
Team Learning	Materials to be learned are distributed with attached questions. The group attacks what must be learned and answered in teams of five to eight.	The teacher either observes the groups as they interact *or* participates in the teaching of the material to be learned and then observes the groups as they interact. The teacher may then elicit the responses of each group and cause the sharing of intergroup information. *or* Either the teacher, an aide, an outstanding student or

a student teacher may participate in the process by questioning the teams as they attack the materials to be learned and the questions to be answered.

or

The teacher may teach what should be learned, as the aide or student teacher circulates between each of the groups to assist when needed.

or

In addition to some of the above, capable students may be placed at vantage points in the instructional area to assist teams that indicate the need.

Circles of Knowledge	A question is posed. Groups of five to eight students respond in rotation.	The teacher obtains the responses of each group at the end of the development period; each recorder deletes from her group's list the responses given by others.
		or
		One adult (teacher, aide, student-teacher) sits with each group at the end of the development period and obtains and discusses its answers.
Group Analysis	A problem is posed to a large group, which is then subdivided into smaller teams of five to eight. Each team works toward the development of alternative solutions.	At the end of the development period, the teacher obtains the responses of each group, and visual comparisons of the possible solutions are made for cooperative analysis.
		or

		The teacher participates in the team discussions of possible alternatives.
		or
		At the termination of solution seeking, one student representative from each team meets with the other team representatives to compare answers and cooperatively develop what appears to be the best possible alternatives, which are then jointly presented to the teacher and the larger group for their perusal.
Knowledge Analysis	Each team's answers to a problem that has been posed to the larger group are analyzed by members of another team to provide for constructive and original suggestions.	The teacher serves as objective referee to insure accuracy of criticism and fairness of approach.
		or
		Students may serve as an impartial jury to determine accuracy and fairness.
		or
		Students may form the first court of appeals and the teacher is the final judge.

Learning in Small Groups

A recent national seminar of teachers, learning psychologists and authorities in the field of group dynamics described learning in small groups as an "important happening" and an idea whose "time has come."[5] The authors agree, but believe that a combination of contracts, independent assignments and various types of effective small-group instructional strategies are essential to meeting the different needs of individual students. This chapter and those which follow are devoted to practical techniques and groupings appropriate to effective individualization of instruction.

---

[5] *Idea Reporter,* Winter Quarter, 1971 (Melbourne, Fla.: Institute for Development of Educational Activities, Inc.), p. 11.

6 ———————————————

Simulations and Role Playing:
Effective Learning Innovations

How to Develop and Direct Effective Simulations

Simulations—structured imitations of real situations, events or problems—usually involve issues, beliefs, confrontations, points of view, attitudes, interaction, decisions and the resolution of problems.

The military and industry have used simulations for some time, of course. The Link Trainer achieved fame as a simulation of flying conditions for pilot candidates, and today's astronauts practice for real flights under simulated space conditions. This procedure reduces risk to those involved and usually is far less costly than training with real equipment.

Instructional simulations can recreate conditions or situations with as many variables as one would expect to find in real life. The teacher and her students can develop simple or complex simulations in a laboratory reflection of life. The recognition and use of relevant material in structured games can bring excitement, motivation, pleasure and *learning* to bored, turned-off youngsters and new insights and creativity to self-renewing students.

Guidelines

Teachers can create effective simulations in any instructional area at all levels if they follow some simple guidelines:

1. Use real events, situations or conditions that are taken from the lives of students, either past or present.

2. Relate the descriptions, directions, problems and issues to those which the students understand and respond to with interest.
3. Involve students, other teachers, parents and anyone who can react to, improve, suggest, sharpen and add reality and intensity to the simulation.
4. Design simulations that involve from five to eight students at separate tables or areas.
5. Create positions and scenarios that involve all of the participants in active roles.
6. Constantly revise those simulations that partially fail to meet the objectives established for them.

Procedures

The teacher should act as "game master," director and chief consultant for the simulation. He can assign groupings and roles, or cause them to be self-selected, in patterns that take advantage of the strengths, interests and relationships among the students. Eventually, student teachers and students themselves may take on the roles of director or consultants to the players at appropriate stages in their development, understanding and maturity.

After distributing the simulation materials to the groups, the teacher should explain the purpose of simulations and the specific objectives of this game in particular. Review what the process can do and what it will not do. For example, specific right and wrong answers or conclusions may not be an expected outcome, but alternative solutions and problem-solving skills may develop among the group as appropriate goals.

Allow several minutes of reading and "warm up" time. The latter is especially important the first few times you try simulations in order to allow each cluster of students to achieve group identity and overcome any apprehension about a new technique that actively involves all of them.

Begin the game and encourage interaction among appropriate subgroups and participants. Join each group for a part of the time and suggest patterns of behavior if necessary.

Follow the simulation with group analyses and class discussion in a variety of patterns, such as team learning or circles of knowledge. Brainstorm the perceptions and criticisms of the game, its results and suggestions for improvement.

Designing Simulations to Meet Instructional Needs

Simulations are particularly appropriate for a number of educational goals:

—Developing problem-solving skills.
—Designing alternative solutions.
—Fostering decision-making ability.
—Training students to cope with confrontations, differing attitudes, problems, decision points, antagonism, anger, confusion and emotions.
—Developing objective insight into reasons, causes, beliefs and behavior.
—Learning techniques of analysis.
—Encouraging participation, involvement, creativity and a desire to learn.

This "gaming" approach is also very suitable as an instrument to meet a wide variety of instructional needs.

In language arts every aspect of communication, from writing newspaper stories to re-enacting the origin of a poem, can be incorporated in a simulation.

Modern issues can be simulated against a backdrop of the past or present in social studies.

Creative personification of geometry figures ("I am a triangle; you are a circle"), job interviews and the application of mathematics to space flight are all fair game for simulations.

Science adventures, animal tales, chemical problems and biological journeys can be simulated.

Multidiscipline approaches, the humanities and training for student government or actual vocations are especially suitable for simulation design.

The design of specific objectives for individuals or groups, the evaluation of the simulation's success and the encouragement of behavioral growth are critical to the technique's success in different instructional areas.

Sample Simulations for Better Learning

I. English and Communication—Suggested Grade Levels 8-10
(Also suitable for Social Studies)

Theme: Poverty

To the Participants

You are about to engage in a simulation designed to challenge your powers of positive thinking and test your ability to write clearly and objectively about an emotional subject.

A perplexing and difficult problem confronts the citizens of Affluent Park, Ohio. A group of your student leaders has demanded that all of the families of the community accept one very poor and educationally disadvantaged youngster into each home for a period of at least one year. All of the families in Affluent Park could afford to do this without financial hardship, but there are strong differences of opinion concerning this method of attacking the social problems engendered by poverty in this country.

In an attempt to ease the emotional climate, the mayor has called a series of Saturday workshop meetings in the schools to discuss the proposal, identify alternatives and find acceptable solutions to the problem of disadvantaged youngsters. As students, teachers, town officials, parents, reporters, citizens or businessmen, you will attempt to resolve the differing points of view and offer plans that the townspeople can support in dealing with the effects of poverty on children. The simulation assignment is to *devise guidelines for improving the social and educational opportunities of children in poor and deprived families.*

Included in the materials before you are an identification badge and a scenario describing your particular role in the simulation. [Each role should be typed on a separate sheet of paper with full identification of the role and the simulation to be played. Role cards (badges) should be worn or displayed by each participant.] Try to make the goals of your group your very own ("internalize" them) and work toward them throughout the simulation.

Format (Time allotment at the discretion of the teacher)

1. Warm-Up (10-15 minutes)—During this period, the purpose of simulations and this game in particular will be explained by the teacher.
2. Round I (25-35 minutes)—Roles will be assigned to participants and materials distributed. Each person will put on his identification badge and read his scenario. Next, the teacher will organize four mixed groups. Each group will consist of one town official (mayor), one reporter, one student, one parent, one community business owner and one teacher, all from Affluent Park, and one poor parent from Meadow Swamp Downs. The remainder of Round I will be devoted to a discussion of possible solutions to the social and educational problems of disadvantaged youngsters.
3. Round II (30 minutes)—As a group with differing points of view, develop a model plan for reducing the effects of poverty and educational deprivation in your community. This model should offer suggestions appropriate to other communities.

4. Round III (30 minutes)—A national caucus is called for *each* group to discuss the very issue that has inflamed your community. Mayors, parents, students, teachers, reporters and businessmen from similar towns all over the country should gather with their role-alike colleagues to discuss the proposal and develop position papers.

Suggested Conference Locations

Mayors	—Hawaii
Reporters	—New York City
Parents	—Grossinger's Resort (N.Y.)
Students	—Washington, D.C.
Businessmen	—Miami
Teachers	—Las Vegas

5. Rounds IV and V (45 minutes each)—As a group, aid the reporter in writing an article that will present your plan(s) objectively to your community and other areas in our country.

General Information   Poverty

THE AFFLUENT PARK TRIBUNE
Thursday, March 19, 1970

STUDENTS DEMAND YEAR-LONG ADOPTION TO COMBAT THE EFFECTS OF POVERTY AND POOR EDUCATION.

Leading citizens of this community today supported student demands that all families "adopt" one poor and educationally disadvantaged youngster for a period of at least one year as a means of combating the effects of poverty and inadequate education.

Mrs. Ima Libbrul, spokesman for the group, said "We must do something concrete to break the crippling pattern of poverty in our affluent society. The students want to take action here and now. If we don't, we will be supporting starvation amidst plenty and revolution at a time when we're trying to promote peace and happiness for all."

A differing point of view was offered by Mr. Ken Survitive of International Machinery, Inc.: "If we turn this country into a welfare state, the individual will lose all respect for his own worth. These students want to give everyone a free handout or a home for a year. Why should they want to learn and work?"

Mayor Voat Expediencia has called a series of civic conferences to discuss and explore this important issue.

(See pages 178 and 179 for photograph and editorial cartoon.)

Photo 6-1. *Photograph by Ronny Jaques,* The Family of Man, *1955.*

This photograph (Photo 6-1) was taken yesterday in neighboring Meadow Swamp Downs. The little girls are waiting for the arrival of the welfare worker who brings their monthly food stamps. They didn't go to school today because they had to stay home to help their mother, who is ill.

"And they bawl me out for spilling my milk!"

Figure 6-1. *GMAC cartoon by Jim Whiting.*

This editorial cartoon speaks for itself when the reader compares it with the photograph on page 178.

Scenario (Confidential to *Students*)   Poverty

You are attempting to influence adults who (you believe) are more interested in protecting their two-car, one-yacht garages than in promoting human values. You see Affluent Park as a symbol of what is wrong with our society. At the same time, you believe that most of the students and some of the parents can do much to change "The Establishment" so that it becomes more responsive to the human needs of all segments of our society.

For the past several months, you and your friends have been promoting a "live in" plan for the poor and educationally disadvantaged to orient them to the values of education and the kind of life one might aspire toward. You are willing to listen to alternative and innovative approaches to the problems of poverty and poor education, but you have little patience with adults who wish to retain traditional approaches to the problems of inadequate education and unequal opportunities.

Scenario (Confidential to *Teachers*)   Poverty

You feel torn between maintaining a neutral position as a professional employee and fulfilling a moral obligation to support the values and attitudes expressed by students and parents who favor the plan to house poor and disadvantaged youngsters in the community. You realize, too, that the issue can become emotionally charged and that the school board and administration might consider this a political and social issue that should not be fought in the schools. You believe that the administration would prefer that teachers not "take sides."

In addition to your belief in the correctness of the student position, you personally have resented the monetary barriers that have prevented you from living in Affluent Park, the place where you work. You decide to support the attack on poverty and poor education with as much objectivity as you can muster.

Scenario (Confidential to the *Town Official*)   Poverty

As mayor of Affluent Park you resent the entire movement to bring poor children into the homes of the community. In the first place, the issue has made the front page of the *Tribune*, where the editor has elected to display photographs of the poor in neighboring Meadow Swamp Downs (an item that could conceivably affect local real estate values). In addition, that formerly responsible newspaper is now running editorial cartoons that disparage and challenge the values of some of our leading citizens.

The situation appears to be getting out of hand, and you fear that quiet Affluent Park may be caught up in a politically chaotic and emotionally charged crisis. Your responsibility is to calm the troubled waters and return your town to its pacific and stable atmosphere. In actuality, you believe that poverty is too complex and broad a problem to be coped with effectively by individual citizens. This is basically the responsibility of the state and federal governments, which will eventually design legislation to care for those poor who never seem to be able to elevate or care for themselves.

Scenario (Confidential to the *Business Owner*)   Poverty

You can't understand this new "welfare philosophy" that has come over everyone. You had to make your way up from poverty, put yourself through school and support your parents as well. Anyone with the desire and willingness to work hard could get ahead in this country. The government spends more and more on welfare and people who are too lazy to hold onto a job.

Now some folks in town want to flood the place with these worthless do-nothings. You believe they'll ruin our beautiful tree-lined streets with dirty, long-haired hippies and yippies who think that the world owes them a living. Furthermore, they'll probably steal and bring drugs to the children in our fair city. These "do-gooders" who want to fill the town with poor trash don't know what they're letting themselves in for, and you strongly uphold that it's our duty to prevent them from placing everyone in danger.

Scenario (Confidential to *Parent of Affluent Park*)   Poverty

You have mixed feelings about the student drive to house poor children in your home and in those of your neighbors. You are apprehensive about the proposed visitor's sense of responsibility to your property. Moreover, what if the poor youngster's repressed hostility wells up in a tide of violence against his benefactor's affluence? Even if he restrains himself in your house, the youngster's resentment might increase when he returns to the ghetto and lead to an organized campaign of destruction in the suburbs.

Despite these felt anxieties, you have been listening more and more of late to your children's point of view and are more receptive to dramatic and far-reaching attempts to conquer poverty in this country. You find yourself uncomfortably sitting on a fence between, "Let George do it" and, "By George, I ought to do something."

Scenario (Confidential to the *Reporter*)   Poverty

There hasn't been so much excitement in Affluent Park since you accepted this position on the *Tribune.* You are not going to let this issue die peacefully. Besides believing in this entire procedure to fight poverty and poor education for some, you have a job to do in keeping this story on the front page. The rich need to be reminded that they have an obligation to all of the citizens of this country. Many of them owe their wealth to their own good education and the sale of items that the poor buy.

The issue is now an emotional one, and the story sells newspapers. If you do a good job, your coverage may get national recognition and you could obtain an even better position. You might even become an editor. Your task is to report the happenings as factually (but as colorfully) as possible. You hope the debate goes on for months.

Scenario (Confidential to the   Poverty
  Parent of Meadow Swamp Downs)

You can hardly contain your anger and hostility. Those people across the tracks really think they're better than you are. Yet they seem to have more drug and family problems than anyone in your town ever dreamed of. More than that, they hide behind a wall of money and want the rest of the world to go away.

Well, your children deserve the same opportunities to attend better schools, obtain good jobs and escape poverty. Why, your children will do better, given half the chance, because they know how to live with problems; the kids over there are given television sets, cars and most everything without working for them.

You've been invited to this meeting over in Affluent Park as a citizen representative of Meadow Swamp Downs. The way you feel now, you're not sure you would even let one of your town's children associate with those snobs. Yet, a year or so over there might give your youngsters the drive and knowledge to climb out of poverty.

* * * * *

II. Health—Suggested Grade Levels 3-6

Theme: Smoking

To the Participants

You are going to play a part in a game. This game will help you understand how other people feel sometimes. We will talk about some of the dangers you may face as you grow up.

Many of the children in your school have been talking about smoking. They noticed that television stations no longer advertise cigarettes. Many parents are trying to give up smoking, and they often talk about the dangers of smoking.

Some of the older children in the school have been coaxing younger ones to try smoking. Some of your classmates are worried, still others are curious and would not be afraid to try to smoke.

Your job is to talk about smoking through the part you play. Plan how you will avoid smoking.

After you read this, your teacher will give you a part or role to play in the game, or "simulation," as it is called.

1. Read your part and wait for directions from the teacher.
2. When the teacher tells you to begin, try to make believe that you are the person in the part you have been given. Talk about how you would feel about smoking if you were really the person in your part.

3. After you have talked about what Jimmy did (Photo 6-2), try to answer the following questions:
   - How did young Jim get the cigar?
   - Did he like the taste or smell?
   - Do most people like the taste or odor when they first try to smoke?
   - Why do people cough when they smoke?
   - Why do people smoke, even though it is not pleasant at first and they know it can harm their health?
   - Do people do other things that are not good for their health? Why? How can you avoid doing the same things?

Photo 6-2. *Photograph by Leonard McCombe,* Life Magazine, © *Time, Inc.*

Part 1 (For the *Father* Only)   Health

You are Mr. Well and you are upset because your young son, Jim, tried smoking a cigar. He's only seven years old. You know he's not a "chain smoker" (a person who smokes one cigar or cigarette after the other) but you think this would be a good chance to talk about smoking with the whole family. You begin by saying, "Brother Bob is becoming quite a photographer. Yesterday he took a funny picture of Jim with his new camera and enlarged it for us. Want to see it?" (Show photo when they say yes.)

Part 2 (For Brother *Bob* Only)   Health

You are happy that you were able to get such a clear and funny picture of Jim. You know, however, that Dad is leading up to some kind of lecture on smoking. You really feel sorry for Jim. After all it isn't as if he smokes cigars all the time. Perhaps you shouldn't have shown Dad the photo even though you're proud of it.

Part 3 (For Brother *Jim* Only)   Health

You feel unhappy that a special family conference is being called just because of that old cigar. You didn't even like it. Why is it such a big deal? You are angry with that older brother of yours. You think he was mean to sneak around with his camera and catch you with the cigar.

Part 4 (For Sister *Jean* Only)   Health

You're glad that someone else is in trouble for a change. You remember when you tried on Mom's clothes and tore her best dress. It's nice to put the spotlight on someone else, but you feel sorry for Jim, too.

Part 5 (For the *Mother* Only)   Health

As Mrs. Well, you approve of these family conferences. Everyone has a chance to talk about what happened and you can solve any problem as a group. You all feel closer afterward. It's difficult for you to keep from laughing when you see the photo, though. You know Mr. Well is trying to discuss a serious matter, but Jim's expression is so funny!

* * * * *

Modifications

These simulation models may be modified, of course, to be used with different types of students and in varied communities and situations. For example, the simulation concerning poverty could be transferred from the suburb Affluent Park to a large city that has disparate sections ranging from upper middle class to disadvantaged. The game on health could substitute drugs for tobacco with appropriate character and dialog changes.

The technique is an important one for bringing relevancy and reality to the classroom and for developing problem-solving skills. Every effort should be made to design simulations that are meaningful to those who participate. Therefore, modifications may need to be made in any instructional strategy you seek to use in your classroom.

Advantages of Simulations

Simulations remove the threat of reality. Inhibitions, tension, fear and anxiety are usually left behind once the participant gets into the "game."

Most students and people who join simulations gain new insights into the motives and behavior of other people. Players are forced to take positions and play roles that may be different from their own. Understanding usually increases greatly when this occurs.

Simulations provide pleasure, excitement, stimulus and a change from the usual pattern of learning skills or information. Thus intensity and variety, two of the key elements in learning (see Chapter 1), are both present in this teaching strategy.

Real issues and elements are presented. Relevance and reality make the simulation highly desirable as a teaching strategy.

Simulations increase motivation because all students are actively involved in relevant group learning situations.

Situations, confrontations and decision points are built into well-constructed simulations. Numerous opportunities to provide alternative solutions, develop problem-solving skills and foster decision-making ability are easily designed into any simulation.

Designing Role-Playing Techniques

Role playing features a fairly unstructured, spontaneous and immediate response to certain situations. Problem solving and decision making are not central to the process.

Pantomime. Pantomime is particularly appropriate for the elementary school in an informal learning activity, while it may be more suitable to the upper grades in a more structured situation such as a formal play. Once the younger students become familiar with the technique, you may be able to give the directions in pantomime.

Pantomime can be attempted by one youngster or a small group for the entire class, or by several youngsters in subgroups of the class. Photographs, cartoons or situations described by the teacher or students may be used to initiate role playing in the form of pantomime for most subject areas.

Dramatic scenes. An infinite number of instructional situations lend themselves to role-playing various dramatic scenes. Some examples for the primary grades might include:

Halloween Night	School, Ugh!
The Dentist's Office	The Picnic
The Firehouse	My First Airplane Ride
Fire Drills	The Bully
Lost!	Keeping a Pet in School

The teacher may assign roles or have the students design and select them. At times, the teacher may have to ask questions or list some goals on the board to keep the group moving toward its objective.

At the secondary level, improvised dramatic scenes may be motivated by the interests expressed by students; e.g.,

If Romeo and Juliet were alive today.
My first date.
"Try one. Are you chicken?"
"Yes, Mr. President?"
"I am your friendly, neighborhood guidance counselor."
TV or no TV?
"You kids shouldn't be allowed to drive, vote or drink until you're at least 25."

Living history. Some preliminary research into various past situations and events can aid in making history live and have relevance for our times. In the middle and junior high grades, for example, it would be very useful to have groups of students assume that they were living at the time of an event under study. Roles may be assigned and some of the actions and reactions may bring the past right into the classroom.

One illustration of this approach might be the re-enactment of the Boston Massacre. Some reading and speculation about what things were like in Boston at the time would reveal that the British soldiers billeted in Boston were hated, feared and unwanted. Their bright red uniforms earned for them the derogatory term "lobster back." In all likelihood, they were not pleased to be far from home and surrounded by hostile citizens. Some youngsters, perhaps the same age as those in your class, undoubtedly found the "lobster backs" inviting red-coated targets for snowballs in the winter. A gun fired by accident, or in earnest, might have precipitated the tragic incident of those who were thought to be provoking or threatening his majesty's troops with rocks—or snowballs! A number of roles could be established to depict and *live* this situation. "You are there" could happen at any time, for any age.

Value situations. Various approaches can be used to develop roles based on value situations. Photographs or drawings may be used to focus attention on attitudes and values, and roles may be assigned at different levels.

Primary—Everybody Plays with the New Baby.

Scene 1—Unhappy Situation (Photo or Illustration)

> Grandmother and grandfather arriving in car
> Father holding baby aloft
> Mother coming with bottle
> Both ignoring petulant four-year-old

> (Assign above roles)

Four-Year-Old Optional Roles

1. You could cry.
2. You could break your toy.
3. You could play with the new baby.
4. You could say, "Play with me too!"

Discussion of Four-Year-Old Role

1. Crying will not make you happy.
2. Breaking your toy will make you cry more.
3. You could play with the baby.
4. You could say, "Play with me too!"
5. You could play with the baby and also say, "Play with me too!"

Scene 2—Happy Situation (Photo or Illustration)

> Four-year-old on grandfather's lap
> Grandmother showing baby to four-year-old
> Father and mother in circle giving approval
> (Replay scene)

"We have, your honor!"

Figure 6-2. *Cartoon by Gustav Lundberg.*

Secondary

1. Assign the roles illustrated and dramatize aspects of the attitudes and values we hold toward women and the jury trial.
2. Use the cartoon (Figure 6-2) as a rallying focus for a group of women's liberation advocates.

Advantages of Role Playing

Role playing aids students in gaining insights into behavior. Whether the student identifies with a role or not, the technique forces him to feel or "think" the part of the person he is playing. Except in cases where he may block out what is really happening, the student will increase his ability to understand the reasons for what people say and why they behave as they do.

Having someone else say things a child believes in or disagrees with will aid him to understand situations, problems and issues in ways he had not thought of before. Playing different roles requires new analysis or fresh viewpoints and assists the student to develop new perceptions.

Hostility and aggression, as well as joy and spontaneous energy, can be released through the creative outlet of role playing. Invariably, children begin to look forward to the "fun" of role playing. Additional acclaim or reward may be obtained through recording the role-playing sequence on audio or video tape.

Creating or playing a part can lead to rational understanding, desire and motivation to change behavior. The maturing process is often aided through the multiple mirror of role playing.

It is often difficult to develop values because of the lack of appropriate and optional examples. Role playing allows the exploration of situations and attitudes in depth and from many vantage points. Values can be built on the situations depicted and discussed.

"Experiencing" an incident before it happens can bring invaluable training to all students because everyone must face certain situations and problems. The safe environment of a dramatic scene is usually much more appropriate in preparation for actuality than a lecture, written description or discussion.

How Role Playing Differs from Simulations: Appropriate Applications for Both

Role playing involves the spontaneous and less structured use of real or imaginary situations. Single incidents, current attitudes, feelings, values, issues and an instantaneous response or dialog give role playing its dramatic strength and relevance.

Simulations, on the other hand, are structured, defined in advance, game-like rather than essentially dramatic and designed to develop decision-making ability and problem-solving skills. Roles may be played within the framework of the simulation but usually are intended to contribute to the understanding of issues, problems and attitudes as the participants seek alternate solutions to problems.

Some Applications

Simulations	Role Playing
How Can Our Community Cope with Local Poverty?	The Job of the Policeman (Fireman, Postman, Teacher, etc.)
What Are the Qualities Our Next Principal Should Have?	How Should We Behave on Our Class Trip? (The bus, etc.?)
What Are Some Improvements We Could Bring into Our Schools?	Acting Out a Story We Read
	A Television Program I Like

Some Applications

Simulations	Role Playing
How Can We Learn to Control Our Tempers?	My Birthday Party
	On a Date
What Are Some Things We Do to Improve Our World?	When Someone Moves into Our Neighborhood
How Can We Overcome Pollution?	When I Want to Correct My Teacher: Ways of Saying Things
What Can We Do to Understand Each Other Better?	My Parents Don't Understand Me
	The Things That I Worry About

These applications are not necessarily mutually exclusive and, as indicated, roles are often played within the simulation structure. Role playing, however, provides the individual with a vehicle for expression, whereas simulations are used to bring several people together to seek solutions to a problem involving all of the participants. Both strategies involve students in ways that stimulate the desire to participate, express themselves and learn.

7

Brainstorming and Case Studies: Mental Power Released for Problem Solving

Why Brainstorming Can Be Equally Effective as a Teaching Tool or as a Real-Life Problem-Solving Device

Brainstorming, like the other teaching strategies described in this book, easily qualifies for the list of three keys to learning: frequency, intensity and variety. As a learning tool it can be acquired quickly and repeated often at appropriate intervals.

Brainstorming is an intense experience that is strongly focused on a single topic for a limited period of time. It provides a very different and stimulating student interaction procedure—the kind of variety that most groups enjoy immensely. Finally, the unleashed and concentrated mental power generated in a brainstorming session guarantees both individual and group achievement as well as any device used or observed by the authors.

All of the teaching strategies in this section are "triple threat" techniques. They may be used: (a) to improve the teaching-learning environment of all students; (b) to develop effective teacher or supervisor training programs; (c) to solve instructional supervisory or organizational problems.

It is in the problem-solving area that brainstorming probably succeeds better than any technique yet devised. The strategy was first utilized in industry as a means of overcoming obstacles, solving problems and finding new and creative approaches to unsatisfactory or inefficient procedures or systems.

The concept is very simple. A group of employees (or students) is given a single problem or obstacle and asked to "storm their brains" for ideas. To increase spontaneity and rapidity of ideas, each participant is encouraged to call out his thought the instant an opening presents itself. Each brainstorming session usually intensifies into an exciting rapid-fire, off-the-top-of-the-head group experience. Stimulation and motivation build as each participant contributes and interest mounts to higher and higher levels.

The ideas generated tend to serve as catalysts for new responses. Creative and effective thoughts begin to evolve from this group process. In contrast, individuals often react in traditional patterns and rarely have an innovative "brainstorm" without the stimulus of multiple sounding boards.

How to Design Productive Brainstorming Sessions: Five Questions to Better Solutions

The teacher or student who acts as a group leader should not enter the *process* of brainstorming except as a facilitator. He or she records the ideas on a chalkboard, on an overhead projector or upon large sheets of project paper (30" x 36") with a magic marker. This last device is preferred for several reasons: (a) a permanent record of exactly what was said can be retained indefinitely; (b) typewritten copies can be transcribed at convenient times with minimal effort; (c) a visual record of all ideas, parallel thoughts, project proposals, next steps, etc., remains in view to stimulate new thoughts; (d) an impressive list of ideas, suggestions and procedures builds up in full view of the contributors, thus enhancing their sense of individual and group achievement; (e) involvement and group ownership of ideas become more complete as the participants watch their growing lists.

To begin, the group leader should arrange the participants in a semicircle facing several large brainstorming charts that can be pretaped to the wall. He should introduce the technique by asking the group to call out synonyms for a simple noun such as "leader" or "abode." The group is timed at 2 minutes and is always amazed that collectively they can call out from 20 to 40 words in that short time span. It is impressive (though not necessary) to ask several individuals to work up independent lists during the same 2-minute period in another room. The lists, individually or collectively, usually fall far short of the brainstorming group's effort.

As the participants proceed through relatively few sessions, facility and competence grow rapidly. It is necessary to repeat and reinforce some simple ground rules during the orientation period:

1. Each participant is encouraged to call out his thought or suggestion as soon as an opening (group silence) presents itself.
2. The group is reminded to focus or concentrate on the specific topic, question or issue before the group—*and on nothing else.*
3. No analysis, editorial comment, negative criticism or "put downs" are permitted.
4. All suggestions and ideas pertaining to the topic are written whether they seem realistic or "far out."

The group leader facilitates the process by keeping the group on target, synthesizing responses and asking for clarification when necessary as he records. He may also request repetition or a temporary "slowdown" if the ideas being called out cannot be recorded as fast as they flow from the participants.

After the orientation sessions with simple synonyms, the group is asked to respond to a problem usually posed as a question. It might be: (a) Instructional: What are the similarities (or differences) between customary family life in the United States and India? (b) Problem-solving: How can we improve homework assignments? (c) Training-oriented: What are some instructional techniques that will improve the teaching-learning process?

It soon becomes clear that a wealth of commentary must now be analyzed and restructured to be of real use to the group—especially if the topic is a problem or training device.

Instructional questions can be analyzed readily by the teacher for evaluation objectives, or by subgroups of the class for reporting and reinforcing purposes.

One technique that builds a progressive analytic structure into the brainstorming procedure is the alternating series of three positive and two negative questions. The first brainstorming question poses the problem in the form of a positive question or open-ended statement of what conditions should be in an ideal program:

"School should be a place where _____ ."

The second question asks the group to describe what is preventing these ideal conditions:

"Why doesn't your school resemble the place you described?"

The third question requests some general programs or projects to be listed that create the situation, conditions, school, etc., described in the first list:

"What programs would make the schools a place where _____?"

The fourth question reverts to the negative again in asking the participants to list the obstacles to the successful completion of the programs, wherever they exist, in the school, in society or in themselves:

"What will prevent us from succeeding?"

Finally, the key positive question is asked:

"What are our next steps?" (What can we do individually or in teams the minute the brainstorming session ends?—tonight? tomorrow?)

Each question deserves one or more sheets of project paper and may be numbered from Column 1 through Column 5 for ease of recording and reproducing. In summary then, the questions alternate from positive to negative and become more and more specific.

Column 1	Column 2	Column 3	Column 4	Column 5
The question, issue, problem, goal.	What has caused the situation or thwarts our purpose?	Which projects or programs might we institute to reach our goal?	What will prevent our reaching these goals?	What are our next steps?

Two suggested series follow as examples:

Column 1	Column 2	Column 3	Column 4	Column 5
Homework assignments should____.	What is wrong with current assignments?	What projects or programs could we mount to improve assignments?	What will prevent these projects from succeeding?	What are our next steps?

Column 1	Column 2	Column 3	Column 4	Column 5
Our science program should _____.	What are the weaknesses in our science program?	What projects could we begin to improve science teaching and learning?	What will prevent us from succeeding?	What are our next steps?

Placing the Group

Several groupings are possible, depending upon the number of people involved, the facilities, media used, etc. In general, a tight semicircle around the leader or facilitator helps to provide the involvement and cohesiveness necessary for productive sessions, such as shown in Fig. 7-1.

Analyzing the Results

Categorizing the brainstorming notes, setting priorities and acting upon agreed-to next steps are critical to any positive action that should result from the brainstorming effort. The actual parent, student, teacher brainstorming notes list which follows on page 197 (Figure 7-2) was set into a priority goals grid (Figure 7-3) at subsequent follow-up meetings.

Priority Goals Analysis

Begin by establishing a rationale or set of criteria for setting immediate and long-range goals in order of priority.

The brainstorming group agreed on these:

1. Value to students.
2. Attention to methods.
   Recognition of the learning process as a criterion.
3. Feasibility of achievement.
   Financial acceptability to community, students, staff.
4. Numbers of students affected.
5. Legislation (flexibility but with permission).

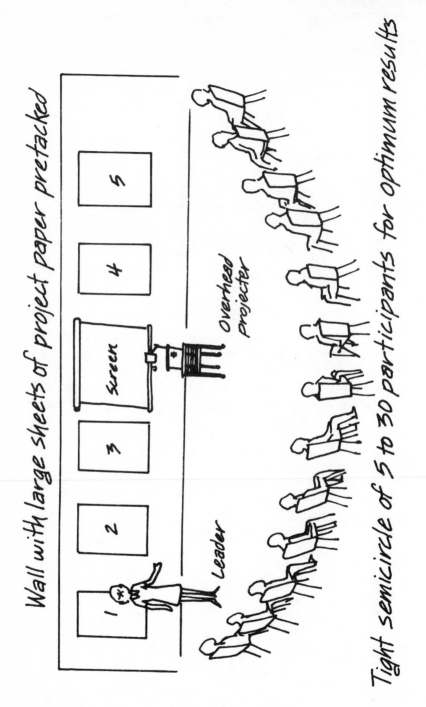

Figure 7-1

With these criteria in view, the group then "voted" by assigning a first, second, third or no place to all of the goals listed under the first question, "Which aspects of our educational system do you feel require improvement?" Three points were awarded for first-place votes, 2 for second and 1 for third; the results:

Brainstorming Notes

Which Aspects of Our Educational System
Do You Feel Require Improvement?

Art—elementary and junior high school
Catching problems early
Ability grouping
Physical education—especially for non-
    physical
Follow-through on problems
Interest to children
Marking system—honor roll
"Busy work"
Music
Pressure—grades—no grades
Different subjects needed
Teaching kindergarten
Coordination K-12

What May Prevent Us from Achieving These
Improvements?

Lack of money
Lack of space
Attitudes of teachers, parents and students
Apathy
Lack of appropriate training
Tradition
Lack of planning time
Poorly planned meetings
Defensive attitudes
Internal conflicts
Staff may not consider it important

What Suggestions Do You Have to Achieve
These Changes?

Art and music—more time, space, staff
Outside guidance
Dance, gymnastics, individual sports—physical edu-
    cation secondary
Reduce class size
More qualified volunteers—music, art, etc.
Adjustment of time and schedule, content,
    expectations
Study marking system for alternatives.
Supervision of teachers—classes should
    be more interesting
Team teaching
After school—extend school day
Supervision of teachers—extend school day
Visit schools, exchange students, attend legislative
    hearings
PTA study class trip possibilities
More contact among school faculties—different
    subject disciplines
Science participation should be earlier and more
    extensive
More use of industry resources—personnel and
    equipment
Local political speakers
Campaign participation by students
Consult with guidance regarding amount and
    kind of activity

Figure 7-2

What May Prevent These Suggestions from Being Realized?

Insecurity of some staff members
Budget development and vote
Negotiation procedures
Inertia
Types of personnel
Closed attitudes toward openness
Importance of conflicting priorities
Lack of communication
Competition for colleges

What Are Our Next Steps?

To evaluate present program in its entirety—right courses, who determines?
Evaluate present art, music, add more money?
Study using administrative regulations
More and better public involvement
Get off campus more—independent study
Foreign languages—pay as you go
Expand after-school activities
Study and evaluate programs
Coordinate trips—industries, etc.
Seek community resources—arts and crafts
More volunteers—(legal problems)
What should elementary school provide?
Study length of school day?

Figure 7-2 (Cont'd)

Priority Goals Grid

	1	2	3	Point Total
1. Coordinate K-12 (interdisciplinary approach, vertical and horizontal)	7	6	1	34
2. Diagnose learning problems early	7	5	1	32
3. Follow through on prescriptions	5	4	4	27
4. Marking—honor roll, class rank, pressure, grades	3	6	1	22
5. Interest to children	4	2	3	19
6. Nongraded, different grades, different subjects	2	4	1	15
7. Ability grouping	2	3	4	14
8. Continued improvement in science, foreign languages	1	3	4	13

Figure 7-3

9. Eliminate busy work (elementary)_____	2	3	1	13
10. Art—elementary, middle school_____		2	1	5
11. Physical education problems (nonphysical) _____		1	2	4
12. Music—more comprehensive (elementary and up)_____			3	6
13. Kindergarten curriculum_____			3	6
14. Visits to other communities _____			3	6
15. Outside speakers_____			2	2
16. Student exchange_____		2	4	8
17. Job training_____		4	1	9
18. Class trips_____			3	3
19. Entire curriculum program_____	1			3

Figure 7-3 (Cont'd)

It was then decided to combine the "next steps" brainstormed at the first session with practical solutions developed after agreement to concentrate on the eight items with the highest scores. The preliminary solution procedures included these suggestions:

1. Improve written communication.
   Send news of meetings, agenda, etc., out early to all concerned, including the community.
2. Communicate expectations and objectives to students.
3. Coordinate all K-12 activities.
   Involve the assistant superintendent for instruction in this task. Establish K-12 subject discipline committees, joint meetings. Schedule visits by staff members among all schools.
4. Use student talents.
   Nominate students to student-faculty councils and curriculum study committees.
   Institute diagnostic techniques—testing, student interviews, student appraisal, aptitude.
5. Use community resources; expand joint adult-student continuing education program.

These involvement and organized planning techniques generally take less time and result in more productive action than the usual types of meetings that serve more as forums for individuals, or obstacles to those who desire responsible change.

*Alternate Methods for Establishing
a Rationale for Setting Priorities*

Basic questions should be posed to the brainstorming group concerning the rationale underlying the proposed goals. What is the *purpose of* or *need for* the suggested programs? Indeed, "Why are we doing this?" should be asked *first*.

Other questions such as, "Is this activity more important than others we should be undertaking?" "Why?" should be next. Questions concerning feasibility, allocation of resources, apathy, etc., should be deferred for discussion and planning when examining procedures.

Another stimulant to practical analysis involves alternating three basic rationale questions:

1. Why should we undertake this project, method, approach, etc.? (What is the need?)
2. What is the nature of the project, course, subject, set of procedures, etc.?
3. Who will benefit? Who is involved? Who will participate, etc.?

Although this sequence seems logical, alternating the order of questions can move a group out of its lethargy, or two subgroups away from impasse. For example, if a brainstorming group begins to draw blanks concerning items of need to establish priority activities based on purpose, the group might attack the question, *What* should we do? (teach? begin? plan? etc.) and *then* ask *why* they are doing it. This reversal can unblock the logjam of ideas, or reveal the reasons for attempting a program, by bringing everyone closer to the specifics of the project before asking them for the basic purposes underlying the action taken.

In the same way, by first asking the group about the people who will be involved, or who will benefit, sometimes may lead to priority actions and purposes more easily than the logical sequence of Why? What? and Who should be involved?

Three Samples Tailored to Instructional Objectives

It is highly desirable to involve groups of students in the selection of their own topics of study and in the choice of procedures to reach their objectives. (See Chapters 3 and 4 on contracts.) Brainstorming can lead to a number of themes or ideas that are suitable in a variety of subjects or multidiscipline topics, such as the examples that follow:

I. *English—Grades 6-8*

  A. Instructional Objectives

    1. To learn to work productively as part of a writing team in analyzing a problem and its possible solutions.

    2. To contribute to the group effort according to abilities and interests. (Each student or group will indicate his/its role in the project.)

    3. To produce a clear, informative group report that contains the following elements:

      a. Definition of the problem.

      b. Alternate solutions considered.

      c. Reasons (rationale) for the solution(s) selected.

      d. A set of logical steps or procedures that you and other members of the group may follow.

      e. Predictions of or applications for what may result.

  A minimum rating of 85 must be attained on all elements of style, ideas, organization, wording, grammar, spelling and punctuation.

  B. Introduction—Selecting a Problem or Obstacle

    Use a photo or cartoon on an overhead projector to motivate the discussion (Figure 7-4).

"Didn't you hear us ring?"

Figure 7-4. *Cartoon by Reg Hider.*

Sometimes problems or obstacles can frustrate us to the extent that we would like to batter aside all resistance as the family in the cartoon did to gain entrance. On the other hand, the homeowners do not seem to approve of the method used by their unwanted and uninvited guests.

C. General Assignment to Students

It is important that students learn to find solutions to problems that are acceptable and effective and that involve all of the people concerned. Select a problem or obstacle that you believe could be submitted to one or more groups in the class for a brainstorming session. You might select a topic from your own background, society in general or your readings concerning American problems. Some samples follow:

How can we end the war?
What can we do about pollution?
How can we help to end poverty?
How can I be more enthusiastic about life?
What could be a "relevant" curriculum for us?
How can I make friends?
How can I avoid getting involved with drugs?

D. Brainstorming Groups

Have the class divide itself into four or five interest groups to pursue joint topics, utilizing the brainstorming techniques described earlier. (Several training sessions should precede use of the brainstorming procedure by groups of students.)

E. Analysis

Each brainstorming group should organize itself into a task team, with roles assigned by the group according to interest and ability. Recorders, editors, proofreaders, researchers, writers, production managers, discussion leaders and critics are some of the roles that may be assumed by the participants to complete the assignment.

Procedures described under "Analyzing the Results" (earlier in this chapter) are used after appropriate training. The group should be required to defend its written report to the rest of the class.

II.   *Social Studies—Grades 9-12*

A. Instructional Objectives

1. To train powers of observation.
2. To use group interaction to form accurate conclusions.
3. To produce a clear, concise argument through the citation of observable evidence for the validity of your conclusion.

A minimum of ten observations of which eight are correct must be attained on the final group report.

B. Introduction—Learning to See

Isolate the faces in the photo imediately following, on an overhead projector, by covering the remaining areas with cardboard or paper. Ask the entire class to brainstorm the emotions they "see." Record the results.

C. General Assignment to Students

It is important to see things in context and observe every detail for possible clues to the truth in a photo, painting, writing or other form of human expression and communication.

Write a short description or narrative about the following photograph.

D. Brainstorming Groups

Have the class divide itself into three or four brainstorming groups in order to build an observation analysis and report on Photo 7-1 entitled, "Barbed Wire."

Assist each group in building a list of questions that they can brainstorm as they look for evidence in the photograph; e.g.:

1. Where was this picture taken? Why?
2. In which country or region did this event take place? Why do you say that?
3. What kind of group is this? How do you know?
4. What are the emotions expressed here? Why are you certain?
5. Who or what is on the other side of the barbed wire? Why do you say that?
6. Are the girls prisoners? Why or why not?
7. What are they wearing? Is this important? Why?
8. What can you tell from the background in the photo?
9. Why are there different expressions on the girls' faces? Is there a difference between those at the front and those toward the rear? Why?
10. When was this picture taken (within 15 years)? How did you come to that conclusion?

E. Analysis

Each brainstorming team should complete the assignment of listing 10 observations, based on the teacher's and their questions about the photograph. Each of the observations should be supported by a written statement of the evidence supporting the observation, as agreed to by consensus. A research project may be initiated by the group if it elects to do so. Each group should be required to defend its statement of evidence to the rest of the class.

III. *Science—Elementary, Intermediate Grades*

A. Instructional Objectives

1. To be able to design an experiment correctly when given a problem to solve.
2. To follow through on team and individual assignments.
3. To cite procedures, results and conclusions clearly and accurately.
4. To observe possible reasons for expected (or unexpected) results.

   A minimum of 90 must be attained on 1, 2 and 3. Evaluation of 4 will be made jointly by the teacher, class and brainstorming group, with honors credit given to individuals and groups for accurate, valid reasons.

B. Introduction—The Scientific Method

Review experimental procedures with the entire class by using a demonstration or an experiment recently completed by the group.

Photo 7-1. *Photograph by Michael Rougier,* Life Magazine,
© Time, Inc.

C. General Assignment to Students

   1. Which freezes first, hot water or cold water?
   2. Design an experiment that will test your answer to this basic
      question.

D. Brainstorming Groups

   Divide the class into four or five brainstorming groups and have
   them decide jointly the steps of the experiment. Brainstorming
   should yield a number of alternate procedures that should be
   analyzed and reduced to one or two steps or approaches. Procedures
   should be tried at home and in school; some students may elect to
   research the topic as well.

E. Analysis

   Each team should write about and report its experimental design
   procedures and results to the other groups and lead a discussion with
   at least one other group on the validity of its results and reasoning.

Several groups may interact at one time when focusing on a single problem.

Advantages of Brainstorming

The advantages of brainstorming are many—as cited by teachers and students who have used the technique. According to experienced users of the procedure, brainstorming:

1. *Is stimulating and provides a varied instructional approach.*

   It generates enthusiasm and eagerness to join in by its open invitation to participate and its rapid, free-wheeling approach.

2. *Is highly motivating.*

   Students who usually allow their verbal, articulate classmates to dominate question-and-answer periods get the urge to participate. They are not "put down" or degraded for "wrong answers" and feel a real sense of contribution as their suggestions are noted on the project sheets. On the other hand, those who dominate traditional classroom situations are also stimulated to get their ideas out and on the record.

3. *Increases "task focus."*

   The brainstorming group is kept on target with very little pressure from the group leader because of the structure and ground rules. Editorializing, personal commentary, rejoinders, eloquent speeches and the other destructive activities of committeedom are eliminated in this process.

4. *Promotes spontaneity and creativity.*

   The members of the group begin to link ideas and "bounce suggestions off the group" in a sounding-board procedure that gathers momentum as the session continues. Mental power is fully unleashed in this positive atmosphere.

5. *Is efficient and productive.*

   Scores of ideas and suggestions or problems and obstacles can be listed in a few minutes. Parallel suggestions and obstacles lead the group toward sound "next steps."

6. *Involves participants in the ownership of ideas.*

   The participants feel greater kinship for their product as they assume group ownership of their ideas and suggestions. Problem solving is made much easier when communal commitment is guaranteed.

7. *Provides a permanent record and aids in developing solutions to problems.*

   The results of the sessions can easily be reproduced or reused to design alternate procedures and programs for solving problems or meeting objectives. The production of the group takes on value as a permanent evaluation record and as testimony to individual and group effort.

Designing Guidelines for Situations and "Original" Case Studies

The case study technique is a valuable complement to brainstorming. Brainstorming releases bolts of creative brain power, whereas case studies permit slow and gradual development of analytical skills. Training in both, with assists from the team-learning and circles-of-knowledge strategies, can aid individuals and groups to generate creative energy and channel the results into thoroughly scrutinized, logical, effective programs and projects.

Guidelines for Development

Form. Case studies are usually written in the form of "short, short" stories. They may also be written as plays or developed in other media, such as films and audio- or video-taped dramatizations. On occasion, groups may present cases as psychodramas or sociodramas. The use of chronological sequence aids students in grasping the flow of events and dealing more quickly with the issues.

Focus. The case should focus sharply on a single incident, problem or situation. Training in analysis is aided by a high degree of concentration on the reasons that precipitated an action, situation or climate.

Relevance. Reality and frame of reference are critical to the success of this teaching tool. Those involved in the analysis of the case must be able to "recognize" the people and what they do as real or possible. The style of writing should capture the flavor of familiar places, people and actions at (or slightly above) the levels of understanding of those participating.

Motivation. Participation in the development and actual writing or acting out of the roles in the case will stimulate the students to participate. Involving them in the types of cases and the goals will also increase the importance of the activity. The quality of the case presentation, its relevance and importance and the degree of involvement are all critical to the motivation of individuals or groups.

Procedures. Case studies are extremely appropriate for small-group discussion, such as might be provoked by team learning or circles of knowledge (see Chapter 5). The material may be read in advance or at the beginning of a team session.

The leader (teacher or student) has a critical role in not dominating the session and in keeping the five or six participants on target. The recorder should note all appropriate points and check with the group often to verify the accuracy of his notes.

Analysis. Key questions must be developed in advance and others added as the group explores the problem, incident or situation. Questions should begin with simple factual "check points" and move into reasons, motivations and analysis of the subtleties and complexities of human experience and interaction, as well as values, standards and other abstractions. Finally, applications should be designed from the conclusions reached.

The analysis should include questions designed to develop powers of understanding, defining, persuading, proving, explaining, describing, observing, perceiving, synthesizing, abstracting, building and solving. Motives, issues, values, causes, results, comparisons, judgments, conclusions and applications are the grist for this intellectual and emotional mill.

Sample Case Studies

Case studies can involve youngsters of different age levels and academic abilities in a variety of approaches which may motivate them toward desired objectives. *Newcomer,* for example, has been used successfully as a training device for prospective supervisors *and* as a teaching technique to provide analysis and problem-solving experiences for older students in high schools. *War Comes Home* and *Friendship Is Color Blind* can by modified for different age groupings and cross-age sections. All of the samples may be redesigned easily for important topics such as pollution, drugs, violence, poverty, interpersonal relations and others.

I. *The Opinionated Newcomer*

   A. Purpose

      Training for supervisor's or principal's role; problem solving; learning how to interact with people who hold different attitudes and beliefs.

   B. For use with

      Faculty, new teachers, teacher applicants, student teachers or above-average high school students.

Mrs. Marino is a fully certified teacher who recently completed a master's degree in early childhood education at a local university. She has never taught but, rather, earned a bachelor of arts degree 18 years ago, married, reared three youngsters and remained at home until two years ago when she realized that her youngest child was entering junior high school and she would have a great deal of extra time "on her hands."

Returning to school for a master's degree, after many years of absence, Mrs. Marino feared that she might not be able to pass her coursework, term papers and examinations. To her delight, she was viewed as "outstanding" by her college professors in graduate school and consistently earned A grades. She was graduated summa cum laude in June and was accepted for a teaching position in the school where you are the principal.

Despite her background and accomplishments, Mrs. Marino has been causing problems since the first day that classes began. She quietly informed the very young but experienced (three years) Jane Hathaway that she is merely babysitting for her students and is not teaching them. Mrs. Marino also lectured the kindergarten teachers that "time spent in school should be profitable—not wasted! Children can play at home! They come to school to learn." These strongly voiced pronouncements have offended other primary faculty members who believe very strongly that they are teaching their charges effectively.

Last week you called Mrs. Marino into your office to discuss this situation with her. She listened patiently but, when afforded an opportunity, explained that the other kindergarten teachers consistently permitted their pupils to play aimlessly and taught very little. She expressed a desire to "help" these younger teachers "shape up."

Today two parents came to visit you. Each had children in Miss Hathaway's class. They stated that Mrs. Marino's class had learned number concepts and how to tell time during the first week and that their children had only had milk, cookies and drawing in addition to "free" play. You tried to placate them, but they insisted that they want their children transferred to Mrs. Marino's class.

C. Situation

1. What are the key factors in this case study?
2. List the possible courses of action open to you.
3. To whom can you turn for help in solving this problem?
4. Who is "right" and who is "wrong?"
5. What is your position toward Mrs. Marino?
6. What is your position toward Miss Hathaway?
7. What are the basic things to say to the two complaining parents?
8. What are the five steps you will actually take to eliminate this problem?

D. Answer all eight questions.

E. Discuss your answers with the team to which you are assigned.

F. Compare the group members' responses with your own.

G. Either keep or alter your own responses, but be able to defend them.

H. Roles to be played

1. Mrs. Marino.
2. Miss Hathaway.
3 and 4. The two complaining parents.
5. The principal.
6. Additional person(s) of your choice.

Demonstrate what might occur at the conference you plan to hold with these participants.

I. Circles of Knowledge

List the administrative and/or supervisory hints you have learned during this session.

II. *War Comes Home*

A. Purpose

exploration of attitudes and values;
dealing with peers;
coping with frustrating situations.

B. For use with

Students of upper elementary or junior high level.

This photograph appeared in your hometown newspaper and identi-fied the soldiers, including your brother, who is crying in the arms of the man in the center (Photo 7-2). Although the story explains that your brother is overcome with the loss of a close friend (the soldier at the left is writing up the details and examining the dead friend's possessions), many of the students in school have begun to taunt you about what a "baby" your brother must be and "Do you cry a lot too?" It is enough to raise tears of anger and frustration to your eyes, and you want to hit all those who deride your brother, whom you have always loved and respected. You have always looked up to him as someone whom you would want to be like when you grow up, and now you are so upset with your friends and their "dumb" remarks that you are too angry to respond.

C. Situation

1. Recreate the situation in the photograph through discussion and the writing or recording of a scenario or script.

Photo 7-2 *Photograph courtesy of U.S. Signal Corps, U.S. Army. Al Chang, photographer.*

2. Role-play the three soldiers in the photo; then role-play the audience as represented by the other three members of the group watching a play or movie.

3. Reverse the roles of the two groups. Record and compare the comments of both scenes.

4. Why do children cry? Why do adults cry? Is the soldier in the photo a "baby"?

5. How do you think you would react to "friends" who seem to be deliberately cruel and insulting about your brother? What are some things you could say?

6. Have you ever been involved in other situations when adults or other students tried to make you feel ashamed or embarrassed? What are some ways you can cope with an embarrassing or humiliating situation?

7. Possible additional group assignments:

    a. After you have studied this picture carefully, discuss with

reference to specific detail in the photograph, the relationship among these three men. Account for as much as you
can see.

b. Write a narrative or play in which you describe the events
that led to this scene.

c. Using this photograph as evidence, discuss the agony of war.

III. *Friendship Is Color Blind*

A. Purpose

development of attitudes and values;

eliminating prejudice;

developing powers of observation

B. For use with

Students—primary and elementary level

C. Situation

1. Look at the picture (Photo 7-3) carefully. Write (or record) a
list of all of the people in the photograph.

2. Make a list of all of the things in the picture.

3. Where was this photo taken? Why do you say that?

4. Are the boys friends? How do you know? Are they different?
How? Do these differences matter to them? Should they?
Why? Why not? What is really important to friends?

5. What do you suppose the man sitting in the doorway is
thinking? What is the other man doing?

6. Make up a story about the boys. What do you know about
them from the way they are dressed? What do you think they
are saying to each other? Would you like to be their friend?
Why? Can girls have close friends? Is girls' friendship different?
How?

7. Possible additional group assignments:

a. Construct a large wall chart showing photos of friends, how
you know they like each other and what they do for each
other.

b. Make up a play about true friends and perform it for some
of your classmates.

c. Make up a script for a film video-tape or audio-tape and act
out a story about the two boys. Can you get someone to
photograph your acting? Can you make a tape of the script?
Can you show the pictures (film) and play the tape at the
same time? Will some of your classmates come to your
show?

Photo 7-3. *Photograph by Henri Leighton,* The Family of Man, *1955.*

How to Develop Student Analysis Skills

Teaching students how to analyze develops many skills of thinking. Analyzing, in general, requires critical examination of an issue, problem, event or situation through the separation of the elements involved.

Specifically, analysis training provides numerous classroom and out-of-school opportunities for children to think,[1] share their thoughts and *evaluate* their thinking process, so that they may know when their procedures and conclusions are correct and applicable to new situations.

These opportunities should include numerous activities that allow youngsters to develop the following skills.

---

[1] Raths, Louis E., et al, *Teaching for Thinking: Theory and Application* (Columbus, Ohio: Charles E. Merrill Publishing Co., 1967).

1. Comparing and Contrasting

Objects, events, living things, photographs, music, periods, people, actions, ideas, conclusions, points of view, works of art, music, articles, poems, plays, short stories, newspapers, films, actors, things, clothing styles—the list is limitless—may be used within and outside of the school to train youngsters to make astute comparisons between and among objects and ideas.

Questions and activities will vary, of course, according to the level of maturity, ability and interest of the student(s) involved.

Primary Grades. Have the youngster(s) list all of the similarities and differences he can find between

two pets	two rooms	two games
two houses	two toys	two songs

Intermediate Grades. Tell the students to compare or contrast the colors in paintings, leaves, clothing, television screens, magazine photos. Have them disregard shadings of color and identify gradations with the names of colors used for variations from the usual red, green and blue with which they have been familiar.

Junior High School. We can often learn a great deal about the art of writing, and other arts as well, by comparison. Any one of the following comparisons will prove fruitful. Ask the students what the significant differences are and how can they account for them. Tell them to compare the book they read with:

a. Another book about the same time or subject
b. The movie version
c. The television version
d. The play version
e. The comic strip version
f. The dance version
g. The music version
h. Another book by a writer contemporary with the author[2]

Senior High School. "In classical writing, every idea is called up to the mind as nakedly as possible, and at the same time as distinctly; it is exhibited in white light, and lifted to produce its effect by its own unaided power. In romantic writing, on the other hand, all objects are exhibited as if they were seen through a colored and iridescent atmosphere. Round about every central idea the romantic

---

[2] Alan Purves, et al, *A Quest for Questions,* Literature (New York: AEVAC, 1969), p. 31.

writer summons up a cloud of accessory and subordinate ideas for the sake of enhancing its effect, if at the risk of confusing its outlines. The temper, again, of the romantic writer is one of self-possession.

> Sidney Colvin
> Preface to Selections from the Work of Walter Savage
> Landor (Golden Treasury Edition)

Test the accuracy of these distinctions by contrasting one of the poems in the classical group with one in the romantic group. The poems should share a common theme."[3]

2. Organizing, Categorizing and Summarizing

Placing "scrambled" material in sequence; preparing material for a report; placing and sorting objects, books and ideas and abstracting major ideas for presentation in short form all involve important thinking skills.

Primary Grades. Have groups of youngsters place all types of objects into a "grab bag." Then assign teams to sort the items into things that seem alike or that they would use for the same activity. Some of the brighter youngsters should be required to seek different kinds of categories for the same objects or subjects, for example:

Games	*Plastic or Wooden Objects*	*Sports Equipment*
Marbles		
Checkers	Checkers	Baseball
Baseball	Pick-Up-Sticks	Football
Pick-Up Sticks	Monopoly Parts	
Football		
Monopoly		

Intermediate Grades. Have the students write about their experiences at a "photography club meeting" using the facts listed below.

Your friend attended the photography club meeting in your place when you were sick. He acted as "secretary" and managed to take the following notes that you must organize into one paragraph for the school newspaper. In writing the paragraph, exclude any ideas that are unimportant or unnecessary. You are to base what you write entirely on the ideas in your friend's rough notes.

---

[3] *Ibid.,* p. 9.

The meeting started on time.

John Lang of the high school photography club spoke to the club.

Twelve of 15 members attended.

Date: June 1

Time: 3:15 p.m. to 4:30 p.m.

John Lang showed color slides. They were "tough."

The meeting was held in our new darkroom.

Everyone wanted to know how he got such good color on the slides with the clowns and the football players.

Mr. Brown asked if we wanted to visit the high school photography club.

John Lang has had two photos printed in the magazine, *Photography*.

The next meeting will be at the high school.

John Lang said you really have to "see ahead" to tell what will be in the finished slide.

I couldn't think of any questions to ask.

Junior High School. Letters to the editors of newspapers occasionally discuss the activities of students. Read the letter below and write a brief summary of the main points made by the writer in favor of children walking to school. Next, read the letters that are made up in response by four of your classmates and summarize the main points that oppose the original letter writer's point of view.

To the Editor:

Why is it that children today never walk? They are driven every-where—to school, to a friend's house to play, even to the movies.

In my day, children walked to school. The exercise was considered good for them. No one imagined for a moment that the dozen blocks between home and school were more than they could manage, even in the deep snow of an old-fashioned winter.

Today, a city or town that does not supply school bus service, even at great expense, is regarded as behind the times. Then it spends still more money to build huge gymnasiums at every school just to give the children the exercise they should have gotten by walking there in the first place.

One result is that our children are growing up with soft muscles. They get tired easily and are often ill, merely because they are seldom out in the air.

I suggest that parents get together and agree to do no more driving

of children. Let them walk everywhere. Let us end school bus service
and build no more gymnasiums. Let the school pass a new rule: no
child gets to class unless he has walked all the way from home.

Yours truly,
Mrs. R. Jones[4]

Senior High School. Select 20 cartoons from contemporary
magazines. Categorize them into areas of humor. Summarize the
main elements of humor in each category and support your analysis
with specific references to the cartoons, their style, detail, artists'
devices, expressions, etc.

3. Observing, Reporting and Applying

Observing, touching, hearing, smelling, tasting, reporting and
using sense impressions is vital to the thinking process. The ability to
apply gained knowledge in new situations can be creative, practical
and stimulating. The motivation to learn is certainly enhanced by
connections, associations and applications at some removed distance
in space and time from the initial learning that triggered the
application.

Primary Grades. Have the youngsters describe what they touch
in closed boxes where they cannot see, smell or taste the object.
Then have them "guess" what the items are. Record their descriptions and discuss the comparisons with others on the team. Build
their powers of concentration and factual observation.

Intermediate Grades. Have the class locate and demonstrate a
number of optical illusions. Then have teams analyze the reasons for
our "eyes" apparently "lying" to us.

Junior High School. Have three youngsters step out of the
room. Then ask the class (or group) to write in exact detail what the
others were wearing. A variation would be to have a student from
another class rush into the room screaming about the new schedule
for about 10 seconds and ask the same question. Then discuss the
obstacles emotions may place before us when we try to observe
accurately.

Senior High School. " 'Hear No Evil, Smell No Evil.' The word
image is often defined as a mental picture—something seen in the
mind's eye, but an image is not necessarily visual. Images can also
deal with hearing, smelling, tasting, feeling; or with an internal
sensation such as dizziness, hunger or thirst. A specific, vivid image

---

[4] Alan Purves, et al, *A Quest for Questions,* Composition (New York: AEVAC, 1969),
pp. 34, 35.

can be more effective than an elaborately detailed description because the image appeals to the imagination in such a way as to suggest ideas and convey emotions. Discuss the imagery in one of the following poems, answering as many of the questions as possible. Tell how many kinds of images are found and what kind of image is dominant. Explain how the images work. Are they appropriately selected?

"Meeting at Night" . . . . .Robert Browning
"Parting at Morning" . . . . .Robert Browning
"The Solitary Reaper" . . . . William Wordsworth
"I Wandered Lonely as a Cloud" . . . . William Wordsworth
"Dulce et Decorum Est" . . . . Wilfred Owen
"Ode to a Nightingale" . . . . John Keats (selected stanzas)
"Definition of Love" . . . . Andrew Marvell
"After Great Pain" . . . . Emily Dickinson
"A Valediction Forbidding Mourning" . . . . .John Donne
"The Good-Morrow" . . . . John Donne
"Dover Beach" . . . . Matthew Arnold
"He Clasps the Crag" . . . . Alfred, Lord Tennyson"[5]

Case Studies Also Develop Needed Adult Skills

The case study strategy aids the teacher not only in providing numerous opportunities to sharpen students' analysis skills, but also to develop abilities that are important in adult life:

1. Planning and implementing.
2. Solving problems and coping with situations.
3. Setting goals and priorities.
4. Making decisions.
5. Testing assumptions.
6. Developing hypotheses.
7. Designing alternatives.
8. Predicting, inventing and re-enacting.
9. Judging, evaluating and modifying.
10. Explaining, defining and improvising.
11. Describing, proving and persuading.
12. Interpreting, visualizing and applying.

Case studies can be written to develop all of these skills. In addition to answering predeveloped questions, students may be asked to react to or develop alternative decisions, outcomes, variations,

[5] Purves, *A Quest . . .*, Literature, p. 5.

relationships and applications. These alternatives, may, in turn, be analyzed by groups of students.

Advantages of Case Studies

1. Case studies provide a strategy for developing material within the student's frame of reference. The characters, situations and events may all strike appropriate responsive and understanding chords.
2. The approach can be stimulating and meaningful if role playing and identification is fostered with respect to points of view, recognized problems and local situations.
3. The cases offer safe, nonthreatening training vehicles for those involved. Students can "enter" the analysis without direct or real effect on their own situations.
4. A variety of skills and experiences may be brought to bear on a problem through the use of teams discussing, analyzing or re-enacting the case. Learning is heightened by the joint effort and several alternate solutions or conclusions can be analyzed.
5. Case studies provide a vehicle to present differing points of view and perceptions to the group and to build understanding of this important reality.
6. This learning experience can provide long-range time for the development of analysis skills, conclusions, solutions and other learnings.
7. The solutions developed may be appropriate to the students' lives in similar situations.

8

Spheres of Interest: Involving Students in Relevant Learning

Planning a Relevant System of Instruction

Most schools have not even begun to challenge, develop or channel the human resources of this nation's relatively affluent and educated citizenry. Students of normal or high intelligence drop out of schools or drop out of learning and self-realization while sitting in classrooms that have little contact with the social realities of their lives. Skills, understandings and attitudes are blunted by both academic and vocational programs that have little or no relevance to the excitement, stimulation and normal motivation of an active and changing world. The greater crime, however, is the neglected development of the personal values and problem-solving skills, love of learning and each student's ability to seek and acquire knowledge independently.

It would be difficult to locate many programs that transport youngsters into the potential of the present or future, through self-development experiences directly and immediately connected with life as it exists now and as it rapidly changes for the future. Despite the absence of such programs, school and community sentiments are such that the development of humanistic attitudes, self-renewal and problem-solving skills would find wide adult and student acceptance.

Objectives of a Relevant System of Instruction

I. *Societal Objectives*
   —to prevent dropouts in and out of the classroom

—to prevent unproductive conflict with society

—to prevent the continuing waste of human and natural resources

—to promote the self-realization of all individuals and groups

II. *Individual Objectives*

—to develop a love for learning

—to establish a positive self-image as a unique person capable of worthwhile contributions

—to increase personal motivation and commitment

—to train for continuing self- and other teaching

—to elevate expectations for self and others

—to design opportunities for experiencing and creating

—to foster responsibility

—to develop accurate appraisal skills

—to promote a positive spirit of exploration and individuality

—to instill a positive attitude toward acceptance of others and their individuality

—to create an appreciation of and joy for living

—to build a personalized data bank of appropriate and desired knowledge

—to learn how to identify and solve problems and make decisions

—to use and apply knowledge by appraisal, determination of relevant factors, selection of alternate solutions, defense of the selected action, application and implementation of planned actions and evaluation and revision of current systems.

Guidelines

Interact with students throughout the entire process. Students do not want to be part of a faceless mass treated without sensitivity to their individual personalities, desires and concerns. Students want to be important to their teachers and to each other. They want to be liked and respected for what they are and what they may contribute to their society and environment.

It is necessary for teachers and their students to sit together, talk, exchange ideas and offer suggestions before a curriculum can be fashioned and built into a vitally interesting and relevant program (or minicourse) for either an individual or a small group. Interaction between student and teacher will increase the amount of appropriate subject matter as the teacher diagnoses strengths and interests and the student designs a program with the aid of his teacher resource.

Establish and define your terms or talk each other's language. Many people and groups have stumbled on structure and authority.

If a relevant instructional system is to be created, teachers and their students must understand and follow rules and established relationships.

Some of the area questions that require explicit and accepted definition to insure success include these:

1. Who makes the final decision when there is a difference of opinion?
2. How much time may be spent in planning and organizing before decision making is transferred from one participating group (the students) to the other (the teachers)?
3. What is the range of subject areas within which the curriculum may exist?
4. Must there be a consensus among students before a decision can be made? "Must there be a decision that restricts all the students to one selected pattern, or may several small groups of students decide to work within a different operational framework than was selected by the majority?
5. Who will determine the quality of performance? By which standards? Through which evaluative instruments? (Teachers may reserve this right for themselves if they wish. In practice, however, students learn a great deal by participating in the assessment process.)

Up to now, when teachers or teams of teachers attempted to establish a relevant curriculum, they "leaned too far over in the other direction" and permitted students to usurp much of the decision-making authority. As a result, teachers were unable to structure the learning environment and students did not know how. The lack of structure (which was initially viewed as positive) eventually caused a breakdown in both activity and progress. When students began to dissent because "nothing was being done," it became difficult to get "the majority" to agree to any one course and, as a result, conversation was plentiful but learning was not.

Many problems that originally plagued several experimental ventures that permitted students to determine their own curriculum will be avoided by an open and honest establishment of guidelines that clearly indicate the responsibilities and freedoms within which both the faculty and the students may operate.

It is important that teachers understand that students strongly desire learning options, the right to express their thoughts and respect for their ideas. They do not expect, and are not ready to accept, the responsibility for charting all of their instructional studies. Developing a student's ability to become responsible for his own learning is one of the very important steps toward which educators should be working. Although there are some students who are able to assume such responsibility at this time, the majority of our students are not.

Believe in your task—and try to live the concept! Once the teacher(s) has decided how much freedom in the development of a relevant system of instruction she will permit her students, and has clearly established the framework within which she and the students can work cooperatively, she and her students must establish a list of purposes and objectives for the program. Student needs and interests should be considered as well as faculty needs and interests, community concerns, school requirements, research findings and items that may have been gleaned from visits to other schools where such programs have been attempted. If a teacher believes students will learn better when they are actively involved in deciding what, when and how they will learn, he or she should carefully consider any proposal made by students, if it appears reasonable. The teacher can always reject ideas that (to her) do not appear appropriate or feasible.

A relevant system of instruction should be based on student-identified topics that lend themselves to interdisciplinary study. The emerging curriculum should be evaluated against the students' perceptions of reality and constantly revised when students believe their concerns in the area have either diminished or been replaced.

Individualize, personalize and humanize within a sphere of interest. Students have had very little experience with individualization and they tend to form groups and "follow the leader." Do not surrender to the students' need for conformity by permitting either leaders or a "majority" to make decisions that are binding on everybody else. Encourage each student to select aspects of the curriculum that are appealing to him and to form partnerships, teams or groups only part of the time. (Photos 8-1, 8-2, 8-3). Provide many opportunities for youngsters to attempt activities or assignments by themselves, and help them to compete against their own records if they are "mark" oriented.

Continue to analyze each student as he progresses toward established objectives. Vary suggested or prescribed learnings as the need arises through continuing diagnosis. Students often complain that adults are "in a rut"; being apathetic or self-satisfied is not a product of age but, rather, one of attitude. Do not permit students to become conforming or complacent. Keep them moving forward by helping them to be aware of their ever changing interests, and alter their curriculum as their concerns change.

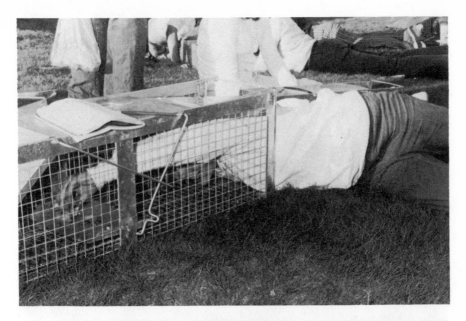

Photos 8-1, 8-2, 8-3. *Encourage each student to select aspects of the curriculum that are appealing to him and to form partnerships, teams and groups only part of the time. (Photographs courtesy of Freeport Public Schools, Freeport, New York.)*

Photos 8-1, 8-2, 8-3 (Contd.)

Create flexible programs and facilities—design multiple options.
Basic to any relevant curriculum are multiple options, alternative
programs and varied responses to individual and group needs.
Curriculum need not necessarily be developed as a course, a unit, a
module, a contract or a topic. Think of curriculum as topics or areas
of interest selected by students in their pursuit of learning—no
matter how lengthy, difficult, enriched, mature, sophisticated or
extensive that area of study might be. Consider the possibility of
minicourses, independent study units that take some youngsters two
days to complete and others four weeks (because they are pursuing
the same topic in varying depths), some programed learning, small-
group seminars, large-group auditorium lectures and demonstrations,
task teams, joint school-community sessions, contracts, multiage
groupings of both long and short duration (dependent upon the

scope and extensiveness of the study), out-of-school learning, "search" projects and seminar weeks where sessions vary in time, breadth and exposure. These are only some of the options for meeting individual and group differences and needs, once the curriculum has been identified by the students and agreed to by the teacher(s). And remember, with teacher guidance, student choice and interest can raise standards and stimulate learning—not dilute them.

Place the responsibility for learning on each individual—help students to be self-renewing. Create opportunities for students to learn independently, assist others and learn in groups. Explore with students the infinite number of ways through which they may learn and grow. Allow them to plan courses, topics, contracts, projects and means of achieving objectives appropriate to their ability and needs.

Develop a series of short tests based on the learnings that may occur through study of the selected programs. Permit (encourage) students to test themselves constantly to determine how much they are learning and/or how much more they still have to learn.

Reward students who work diligently at tasks and whose performance is of high quality. Permit variations of completed programs if it is recognized that change will improve the plan. Encourage youngsters to find new and innovative sources of information, interesting resource people and creative ways of teaching themselves and others. Recognize and flatter talent, creativity and skill.

Make your instructional procedures interesting, important, honest and directly connected to each youngster's frame of reference. Relevance as a term can be overused and oversimplified, but it should never be underestimated. For example, the multimedia and accelerating technology of our generation surround our youngsters in an integrated system of knowledge and feelings. To fragment or departmentalize the disciplines is fast becoming unreal. The only "relevance" left to defend the teaching of isolated disciplines is connected to the habit-developed values of parents who studied subjects that way and who are concerned about change. Integrate the curriculum into large themes, topics, contracts, *spheres of interest.*

Involving Students in the Learning Process

There are many ways to begin involving the students more directly in the learning process. Several are described earlier in the book; e.g., role playing, brainstorming, interest centers, independent contracts, etc. But moving toward sphere-of-interest teaching can begin with some simple procedures that many teachers currently employ.

High School Sample

Identify students who might profit by working with younger students. Establish multiple tutoring teams for youngsters in the elementary school who have learning disabilities. Have each student evaluate the learning style of the elementary pupil, the progress that can be noted and the older student's experiences and growth.

Middle School or Junior High School Sample

Approach two or three of the brightest pupils with the possibility of having them design their own curriculum, based on whatever they recognize as being exciting or interesting to them. Tell them that to find something of great interest, they may use any resource available within walking distance of the school. Suggest, as beginning sources, the library, the high school resource center, local industries, hospitals, agencies, professional offices or other appropriate places that might be used for the purpose of identifying a project of keen interest to them.

They are to report back periodically to the teacher, who will serve as the resource expert who aids them in defining goals and procedures and in evaluating results. Eventually they will "teach" the class what they have learned, using team learning or another appropriate but stimulating technique.

As each student successfully reports that he has found a topic about which he would like to learn, assist him in identifying multidisciplinary objectives appropriate to his abilities and skills.

Elementary School Sample

Request and obtain a bus for a selected class once a week. Involve the parents and other community members in scheduling a series of all-day (or longer) trips to places that will build understandings of the professional world of work, the larger community, government or another appropriate comprehensive theme. Establish instructional goals with the students and parents and evaluate the group's progress *jointly*.

Eliminating Marks, Grade Levels, Schedules
and Formal Subject Disciplines

In the context of our present society, and given the realities of community attitudes toward change and "standards," an educational program is needed at the adult level as well as within schools. Nevertheless, there are positive signs that relevant programs are replacing those that follow a traditional form because it has "always been done that way."

Marks, for example, are being challenged as never before. Many colleges have moved to variations of pass-fail—especially for required courses—and elementary schools have largely changed from A's and B's to S, I and U for satisfactory, needs improvement and unsatisfactory. Teacher-parent-student conferences and narrative reports would be even more meaningful and effective. Finally, self- and joint appraisal would lead to even greater student involvement in self-renewal. Begin by holding teacher-student counseling sessions on problems, successes, strategies to try and self-growth. Soon the marks will seem less important to the student and parent as he moves more deeply into self-appraisal and growth.

Another restriction of relevant curriculums—arbitrary age-related grade levels—is giving way to various ungraded and continuous progress organizational plans. One simple device that can be tried was designed by a Chappaqua, New York elementary school to break the age-grade level pattern. It is called "diamond organization" because one section each of the fifth and third grades are teamed with two fourth grades:

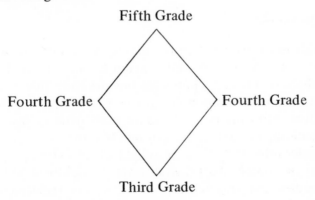

As movement into multiage patterns is made, the grade levels will begin to disappear and interest as well as achievement levels can begin to take their place (*caution:* involve the parents!).

A built-in obstacle, behind which many educators hide, is the block schedule of periods; i.e., five periods of a subject per week at the same time every day. Fortunately, this static approach is being challenged by more and more flexible time patterns, such as the modular schedule, rotating periods, extended labs, independent study, etc. A quicker way to move out of this irrelevant time pattern is to establish project or contract time lines for blocks of work to be completed by the students.

The last (and perhaps the most difficult) pattern to modify is that of formal subject disciplines. Not only is it traditional, but we keep adding more and more "courses" to the catalogs. A beginning step would be to reduce required courses and increase optional offerings. Another would be to identify basic learnings, useful fundamentals and optional knowledge, and to evaluate progress among these after bundling several discipline courses together under a theme or major objective. For example, all of the so-called major disciplines could be taught under a project to modify the transportation systems of the future. Mathematics, science, English and social studies would all be needed, as well as economics, political science, career guidance, art and graphics, engineering and others. Specialists could also be developed within a project team as well as managers, project writers, designers, troubleshooters and politicians.

Critical Guidelines for a
Sphere-of-Interest Curriculum

Definition

A "sphere of interest" curriculum is an interdisciplinary topical study that is of direct and vital concern to the *learner.* By its very design, sphere of interest eliminates the structure that traditionally restricts education to given molds, for no single topic is of interest to every student. Students must therefore participate in designing their own curriculum, for only they can identify the areas of study that are of singular interest to them as individuals at a given point in time.

Letter or number marks, grade levels by age, rigid and repeating time schedules and fragmented disciplines are replaced by broad themes that can encompass multiage groupings, integrated disciplines, relevant topics, active student participation and discovery techniques, independent and group study and analysis, continuing guidance, self-assessment and evaluation that leads to constructive revision and a love of learning and doing.

Very simply, a sphere of interest is an expanded contract theme that can occupy a two- to 10-week (or longer) period of time on a single topic or theme for an individual or a small or large group of students. These are some sample themes that might be appropriate for students, depending upon age, knowledge, interest and ability.

Money	Transportation in the Future
Sports	The Problems of the Cities
Dinosaurs	Changing Moral Values
Space Travel	Pollution and Survival
Drugs	Poverty and Revolution
Racial Conflict	Communication: The Effect of Media
Fairness and Honesty	Human Expression
Pets	The Promise of Technology
Television	Overpopulation and Its Solution
Making Things	Music for Our Times
Wild Animals	Public Opinion and the Law
People I Like	One World
Children of the World	The Bitter Fruits of Slavery
Things that Grow	Work and Play
Building Things	Education in the Year 2000
Experiments at Home	Sports Can Replace War
Scheduling Your Day	Opening a Store
Art Versus Science	Self-Fulfillment Without Drugs
Consumer Economics	Eliminating Ghettos

Procedures

A student or group of students might select a sphere of interest from among those suggested by the teacher or propose one of their own topics to a jury of community residents, university students and others to develop a good, extended study area. A series of contracts (such as those described in Part II) might be developed or modified, depending upon the student's objectives in the sphere-of-interest curriculum.

It is important for each student to define his curriculum objectives clearly so that procedures, the acquisition of appropriate knowledge and skills and the evaluation of progress be continuous and accurate as the student or group of students attempt to fulfill those objectives.

The teacher should meet with the student(s) often to explore ways to acquire the necessary knowledge and skills. It might be appropriate to do library research, attend certain classes, seek tutoring and visit museums, industrial sites, court houses, medical centers, port authority planners, weather stations, office buildings, the mayor's office, universities, etc.

Meetings with teams of teachers, adults and other students responsible for aspects of the developing sphere-of-interest "contract" should be scheduled with the student to aid in the design of next steps, continuing evaluation and revision of plans.

Many of the spheres of interest may overlap among age groups, interest goals, subject skills and knowledge and procedures. These temporary or long-term joint ventures should be planned carefully with the subject-discipline teachers concerned. A sphere-of-interest planning center might provide charts with time lines and industrial planning techniques, such as Program Evaluation Review Technique (PERT), "critical path" or Management by Objectives (MBO). A team of "sphere" teachers might chart some youngsters as shown in Figure 8-1.

Continuing progress and assessment is important to the growth and development of each student. Self-appraisal and group assessment will aid the sphere team and its advisors. Student planning and replanning is equally critical to the student's motivation *and* self-image.

Depth and Coverage

Spheres of interest offer great opportunities for inquiry in depth. Each new question or obstacle requires a search, or problem-solving techniques designed to build each student's ability to learn about and cope with unknowns, as well as enlarge his bank of knowledge and arsenal of skills. For example, questions of law and constitutional government may impede a hypothetical transportation system that links cities and states. However, human relations and sociological problems confront planners who wish to displace people. Anthropological "enculturation" is a formidable obstacle to change. Mathematics, physics, engineering, graphics design, blueprinting, architecture, climate control and a host of other science and technology skills and resources must be brought into the sphere. Reports must be written to communicate. Indeed all of the "disciplines" as we know them today would be taught as part of the sphere-of-interest curriculum.

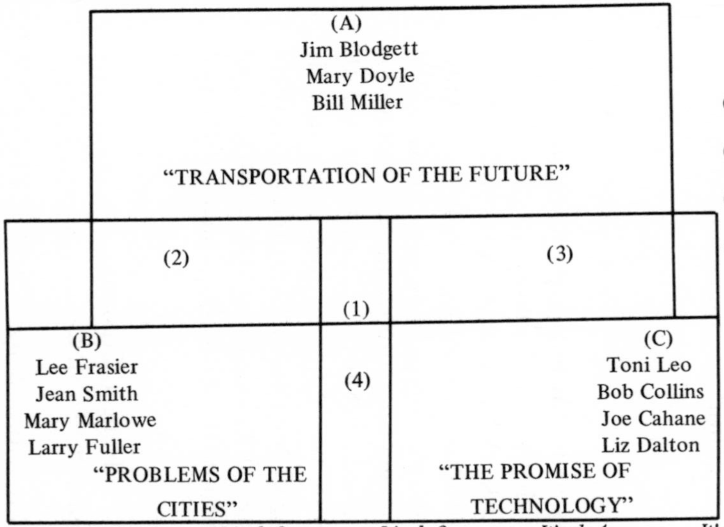

(1) All three teams meet every week to exchange applications that apply to each sphere of interest.
(2) Teams A and B visit the Port Authority and Metropolitan Planning Unit to interview planners and transportation experts.
(3) Teams A and C visit air transportation and military development centers to investigate long-range plans and projections.
(4) Teams B and C work jointly on several aspects of survival and the problems of cities; e.g., nutrition, housing, leisure time, education, communication, power supply and human relations.

(A)
Jim Blodgett
Mary Doyle
Bill Miller

"TRANSPORTATION OF THE FUTURE"

(B)
Lee Frasier
Jean Smith
Mary Marlowe
Larry Fuller

"PROBLEMS OF THE CITIES"

(C)
Toni Leo
Bob Collins
Joe Cahane
Liz Dalton

"THE PROMISE OF TECHNOLOGY"

	Week 1	Week 2	Week 3	Week 4	Week 5	Week 6	Week 7	Week 8
Team A	Develop Objectives, Establish Procedures		Attend Classes, Make Appropriate Visits	Complete Rough Draft		Meet with Other Teams	Reports and Models	Design Final Model
Team B	Define Problems		Develop Objectives	Set Out-of-School Schedules, Begin Visits and Conferences		Redefine Objectives and Set Up New Procedures		
Team C	Develop Objectives		Attend Appropriate Classes Schedule and Hold Work Sessions in the Schools	Set Out-of-School Schedules			Begin Visits and Reporting	

Figure 8-1

233

Relevance

The subject disciplines would be taught as needed and as related to the sphere. They would be appropriate to the interests of the student and essential to the completion of his tasks. Basic fundamentals would not lose their importance; indeed they would be strengthened through a realization of the need to acquire basic knowledge and skills in order to complete successfully a sphere contract of extreme interest to the student.

Continuity

Provision must be made to provide time, space and scheduling arrangements for continuous work on a sphere of interest. Some broad contracts might occupy all of a youngster's time over a period of weeks. Some students may work simultaneously on several briefer or shorter units. Still others might attend clinics and planning units in preparation for the design of a sphere of interest. Many students might pursue their interests through several school years. Continuity is critical to the successful completion of interest-based units of work.

Changes in Behavior

The development of values and continuing, positive growth for each student should lead to changes in behavior as the student matures. Opportunities to work independently and with others should be provided in sphere-of-interest contracts or projects. Success or reasons for the lack of success should be seen and understood by all involved. Several key changes and improvements in behavior should be fostered by the design of and procedures of the sphere-of-interest curriculum. All of these are indicated under the specific objectives listed at the beginning of the chapter. This relevant system of instruction provides the framework; the students and teachers can more easily design the opportunities using the sphere-of-interest approach.

Slow Learner to Advanced Student: Ideas for Spheres of Interest

I. Sphere of Interest—Relevant Education Now!
   Title of Project—Seminar Week

Type of Student—Advanced, High School

Definition of proposed project. A group of bright high school youngsters suggested to their teachers and principal that they would like to plan a series of minicourses that would involve all of the students and the community in a relevant and stimulating period to be known as "Seminar Week."

Procedures. Committees of students planned schedules, sought and obtained speakers and developed a seminar week program of over 300 activities, including nearly 200 "courses" for the five-day period. Outstanding professionals from within and outside the community were invited to participate. Some of them suggested topics, others accepted assignments. The entire high school faculty and administration, the central administration, teachers from other schools in the district and students themselves taught courses or took part in other seminar-week activities. Business firms, utilities and other organizations, as well as nationally prominent sports figures, also participated in the stimulating and comprehensive program.

Six periods of 50 minutes each, with 10 minutes for ". . . discussing some aspect of the class with your teacher" and moving to the next session, were established beginning at 8:00 a.m. Two of the periods were scheduled to allow for a choice of lunch hour, so that each student (and teachers and community members) might attend four courses plus a fifth of featured speakers.

The student-developed catalog speaks for itself regarding what happened after 2:00 p.m., the end of the "normal school day":

> Technically, after fifth period the normal school day is over—you may go. We feel though, that to leave would be crazy. The most significant and noteworthy change found in Seminar '71 is the concept of a live-in, day-long school. This means that at 2:00 p.m. things are just beginning to happen.
>
> The great beauty of this extension of the day is that the campus becomes a truly multidimensional place, with all manner of events and programs occurring. There is now time for dancing, singing and sporting on campus. There will be entertainment, shows and films. Students can spend time painting and changing the look of the campus. And students and teachers will be together for a long day, not just for six hours.
>
> The hours after the courses and speakers are important because in these hours there is no challenge or pressure for homework, no grind of a school environment. The time is spent at fun and on campus. Activities starting at 2:00 and 3:00 include well-known speakers, workshop sessions, bicy-

cling, rock climbing, square dancing, a drum concert and motorcycle rides.

Monday and Wednesday there will be no need to leave for dinner. We will be sponsoring a natural foods dinner and a wedge dinner for those kids who would rather just stay through the evening activities (the cost will be minimal). The evening activities, listed under each particular day, are well worth staying for.

We're asking something unusual . . . during the week of March 15-19, the door to the tiger's cage will be open each day at 2:00 p.m. We're asking the tiger to stay, and find out that he's not in a cage at all.

Community members—Please come, participate, learn and use the school. We have tried to reach you all through one media or another. We want you—it's that simple.[1]

Selected Course Content of Seminar '71 (8:00 a.m. to 1:00 p.m., Monday-Friday)

Africa: A Symposium	Civil Rights: 1970's	History of Folk Music
Peace Corps	Marxist Socialism Comes	Customs and Religion in
Fencing	to the Americas	India
Student Involvement	Stocks and Bonds	Ecology
Technical Theater	Flying	Inventions
Unconscious Education:	Interior Design	Relativity
The Media	Revolutions in Educa-	Minibikes
Campus Art	tion and Life Styles	Multimedia Art
Environment Sculpture	Acting Techniques	Silk Screening
Foods of All Nations	Creative Writing and	The Art of Wine Making
Creative Doodling	the American Novel	Mind Control
Norman Mailer	Poetry Workshop	The Women's Movement
Modern Jazz	Individualism, Taste and	Drugs
Mormonism	Other Matters	Human Evolution
Linear Programing	The Corporation and	Science Fiction
Overpopulation	Business in American	Indochina
Pollution: What Is	Society: A Survey	Yoga
Being Done?	How to Read The New	Opening a Store
Anatomy of a Lawsuit	York Times While	Oriental Philosophy
Religious Potpourri	Half Asleep	Where Are You At?
	Why Was I Born?	

Selected Topics and Speakers of Seminar '71 (Single or Repeated 1:00 p.m. to 5:00 p.m., Monday-Friday)

---

[1] From the Introduction to Seminar '71, Chappaqua, New York, pp. 2, 3.

Technology of Clean Water—Dr. John Anderson, Vice-President of Research and Development, Permutit Corporation.

State Aid vs. City Aid—Mr. Lewis M. Feldstein, Executive Assistant to Mayor John Lindsay on Neighborhood Government.

Radio Free Europe—Mr. Justin Liuba, Senior Editor of the Rumanian Desk of Radio Free Europe.

Sesame Street—Miss Jean O' Connor, Senior Curriculum Specialist for Sesame Street.

The New York Knickerbockers—Mr. Bill Bradley, Forward of the New York Knicks.

Development of New Drug Products—Mr. Chester E. Poetsch, Vice-President and Director of Research Development for Vick Chemical Company and Vick International.

Voyages of Ra I and Ra II—Mr. Norman Baker, Navigator to Thor Heyerdahl.

War Against Crime—Mr. Whitney North Seymour, U.S. Attorney from the Southern New York District.

Peace Corps and Commitment—C. Payne Lucas, Director of the Office of Returned Volunteers, Peace Corps.

What's Ahead for America?—Dr. Walter Judd, former Senator from Minnesota.

Labor Movement Changes in the 70s—Professor David Lewin, Graduate School of Business, Columbia University.

Modern Architecture—Mr. Manfried Hansjoachim Riedel, former Chief Architect NASA Vehicle Assembly Building, Cape Kennedy, Florida.

Chinese Philosophy—Dr. Chih Meng, Director China Institute in America.

Selected Films of Seminar '71 (After 2:00 p.m., Monday-Friday)

Animal Farm	Worth How Many Words
The Family of Man	The Magic Art of Karel Zeman
Ski Pix	How Life Begins
Glass	Lincoln's Last Day
Help! My Snowman's Burning Down	Innocent Years
When Comedy Was King	Cages
Eagle Has Landed	Chickamauga
Rise of Soviet Power	Gandhi
Islam	W.C. Field's Selection
Hinduism	What Right Has a Child
Buddhism	

Selected Field Trips of Seminar '71 (After 2:00 p.m., Monday-Friday)

Lyman Kipp's Studio	Anthony Toney's Studio
Wood Wanderings	Chinatown
African Art	House Tours

| Car Assembly Plant | Pre-Columbian Art |
| County Court House | Picking Up Loose Ends (Rotating Jobs) |

Selected Activities of Seminar '71 (After 2:00 p.m., Monday-Friday)

Evening Sky Show	Natural Foods Dinner	Classical Guitar
Astrophotography	Rock Climbing	Cabaret
West Point Band Concert	Draft Counseling	Income Tax Forms
Cycling	Fiddles and Dancing	Broadway Play
School Within a School	Wedge Supper	Sensitivity Microlab

Obviously, this sphere-of-interest project involved the entire student body and much of the community. The designers, planners, schedulers and coordinators literally created their own and fellow students' educational experience for one week. The benefits and advantages have implications for future jointly planned education of greater duration.

II. Sphere of Interest—Media—Our Last Hope
   Title of Project—Do It Ourselves TV and Films
   Type of Student—Disadvantaged, Slow Learners,[2]
   Middle or Junior High School

Definition of proposed project. A group of teachers, administrators and students mutually and candidly agreed that the usual school experiences, remedial assistance and tutoring simply were not working for a particularly difficult junior high school class. Together they decided on a total sphere-of-interest curriculum based on communication media, such as television, film and photographs. It was agreed that two important objectives would be measured:

1. The stimulation of interest in school and learning.
2. The improvement of verbal and visual communication by the students in the class.

Procedures. Instead of textbooks and written materials, the class first was supplied with Polaroid Swinger cameras, film and art materials. The subjects of photographic "essays" were determined by individual students or two-member reporter teams. Pets, shopping, neighborhoods, the school and pollution became favorite topics. The

---

[2] This sphere-of-interest curriculum is a composite of several successful programs for "slow learners."

equipment became "theirs" on loan for a year; all interest projects and photos became permanent possessions after display and discussions.

Soon after interest in school mounted, a do-it-yourself TV set was introduced into the classroom area. The room had originally been redesigned by the students as a "newspaper office" and was redesigned quickly into a "TV studio." Chairs and desks were moved toward the walls, and space for staging was arranged. The class divided itself into functional committees, such as technicians, scenery, research, script, actors, etc. Most doubled on one or more groups. The initial project was TV commercials, and the new store at the school and school sweaters received a great deal of attention as the finished video tapes were shown on the school's TV sets.

The final phase of this sphere of interest involved film making that carried into a second year for this group. By this time, the camera and television experience of the members of the class brought excited expertise to the art of making short films. The students wrote original stories based on their own experiences. They tried out the dialog on cassette recorders and enjoyed self-critical analysis of what was being said. Words, actions and even intonations that were not "true" to their world were criticized strongly and revised. The films were kept short (3 to 12 minutes) and were polished continually to make them better. Some were shown to other schools and districts and received very favorable comments.

Results. An incorrigible class, one that literally had driven three teachers out of their classroom, had reduced the number of behavior flareups to a few minor scraps between students who wanted very much to contribute. Speech patterns improved markedly for most of the youngsters; the lad who was least intelligible at the beginning of the year won the auditions and became the main TV announcer for commercials and the chief narrator of the films. The usual achievement tests were administered, and despite a minimum of formal training during the two years, scores went up markedly in all areas—including arithmetic!

III. Sphere of Interest—Fairness and Honesty
    Title of Project—What's the Fair Thing to Do?
    Type of Student—Average, Intermediate Grades

Definition of proposed project. Several students became concerned about fairness and honesty. Some parents and teachers appeared to say one thing about a situation and then behaved in a way that did not seem consistent with their announced values. Even more disturbing was the fact that several students appeared to be going down the same path. For example, children were told to admit when they were wrong, but parents never (or rarely) admitted an error. The students agreed to explore ways that would dramatize fair and honest behavior and aid other pupils in coping with problems caused by inconsistent or unfair behavior and in developing open and honest behavior on their own part.

Procedures. A team of four students agreed to interview other students, parents, teachers and the principal in order to identify and categorize a series of behaviors that everyone would recognize as typical and often-practiced inconsistencies and unfair behavior.

Once identified, the team developed a series of flash cards, a game, several role-playing sequences and a set of "What Would You Do?" worksheets.

The flash cards had a series of often-used phrases or sentences on one side and the description of dishonest or unfair behavior on the other. For example:

Flash Card   *Reverse Side*

1 I was only trying to help.	1 Alibi.
7 He started it!	7 Blaming the other guy.
9 Jean's mother lets her stay up till 11.	9 Inappropriate comparisons.
21 But, I didn't hear you call!	21 Selective hearing.

The game resembled *Monopoly* and *Careers*, except that personal satisfaction, happiness, smiles, recognition and growth were the "monopolies" and rewards to be gained. It was necessary to be consistent to pass "Go" and collect two dozen smiles, and only honest behavior kept one out of "jail."

Role playing usually involved other students in situations established by the team. Several skits included such themes as consistency of behavior, favoritism, stretching the truth, unfair criticism, etc. Analysis of what was said in the role-playing sequences followed each skit.

The "What Would You Do?" worksheets were drawings and cartoons that established a sequence of events with a blank box at the end. Each pupil in the class was asked to complete the story sequence and post it on the bulletin board for comparisons and eventual judging.

Results. It was not possible to determine in one year whether the class had become completely honest. The students did become extremely interested in both the subject and the techniques and many more volunteered to help if needed. There seemed to be an increased awareness of ethical questions, and far fewer incidents of negative behavior were reported for that class and school.

Advantages of the Sphere-of-Interest Curriculum

The sphere-of-interest curriculum holds the greatest promise for integrating and unifying learning with regard to relevant and important themes of general and specific issues, conflicts and rapid worldwide change. Classes, marks, grade and age levels, artificial sequences and fragmented subject disciplines can all be eliminated through a sphere-of-interest approach. Out-of-school and community-involved education are appropriate and necessary to the full culmination of this system. The advantages are many:

Interest and motivation. The youngster who wanders about the house pleading "What can I do?" will more than likely have a number of activities at the library, with friends or in the community, which are important to his sphere of interest. The dropout will find himself with a reason to drop in at various centers within the community to work on specific projects or actual jobs related to his program. Bored students at school will have less reason to drop out mentally because they will be involved in projects or contracts of extreme interest to them. Teachers will gain greater professionalism and autonomy as they shift from repositories of knowledge to guides, counselors and facilitators of the learning process.

Importance and relevance. Students will be working on relevant and important topics such as pollution and poverty. Transportation of the future will depend upon the dedicated and creative adults who begin thinking and preparing for the problems of tomorrow today. War, racial conflict, violence, poverty, illness and the other afflictions of mankind must be solved by positive, self-renewing young adults.

Coping and solving. Coping with difficult situations and solving problems cannot be learned unless opportunities and training are provided. Simulations, role playing, brainstorming, case studies and task groups can provide those opportunities effectively, under a sphere-of-interest curriculum that establishes a project consisting of appropriate multisubject disciplines, skills and objectives.

Individualizing and humanizing. This system allows the individual to grow as rapidly as he can and along self-selected paths. Human relations and the importance of interaction is stressed as individuals learn to work with others as well as alone. Independence and interdependence are critical to the self-realization of each child and the survival of the world in which he will live.

In Conclusion

Those of us who believe strongly in individualization hopefully would have every educational program designed to advance the growth and self-realization of each student. Individualization of instruction should progress to the degree that all prescribed learning, will be based on each youngster's abilities, interests, style of learning, rate of learning and achievement.

Students should have the options of working in small groups and independently; with teachers and other adults; with younger and older students. They should be able to study in and out of school buildings; in the community and at places of employment; at museums and in the environment. The community will become the school, and the objectives and studies will vary as each youngster pursues his own "contract." Indeed, Benjamin Bloom poses the theory that slow learners can learn as much as fast learners, but that they require more time and different instructional strategies.[3] The "contract" approach permits flexible time periods for mastery and provides a variety of methods, so that most students (approximately

---

[3] Bloom, B. S., "Learning for Mastery." Evaluation Comment (Center for the Study of Evaluation, University of California at Los Angeles), 1, No. 2 (1968).

90 to 95%) should achieve realistic goals with a minimum of tension and a maximum of self-appreciation.

Competition will be against and for self. Expectations and standards will be even higher than before, and values will be more meaningful as each student builds his own self-image and, through positive interaction, assists others to build theirs. Decision making and problem solving will become the focus of education, not the by-product of it. Students will love to learn, not because an academic degree will advance them economically, but because education will provide each individual with the personal fulfillment envisioned by those who founded this democracy.

Individualization, the process and the method, can achieve all this for your students—through you!

Selected Bibliography and Sources of Additional Information

Allen, Dwight W., and Seifman, Eli, editors, *The Teacher's Handbook.* Glenview, Illinois: Scott Foresman, 1971.

Bishop, Lloyd K., *Individualizing Educational Systems.* New York: Harper & Row, Publishers, 1971.

Dunn, Rita Stafford, and Blum, Hamilton, *Individualizing Instruction.* Jericho, New York: Board of Cooperative Educational Services, 1970.

Edling, Jack V., *Individualized Instruction.* Corvallis, Oregon: Continuing Education Publications, Waldo Hall, 1970.

Engelhardt, N. L., *Complete Guide for Planning New Schools.* West Nyack, New York: Parker Publishing Company, Inc., 1970.

Guthrie, James W., and Wynne, Edward, *New Models for American Education.* Englewood Cliffs, New Jersey: Prentice-Hall, Inc., 1971.

Hartley, Harry J., editor, *Individualizing School Systems: The Elementary and Secondary School.* New York: Harper and Row, Publishers, Inc., 1971.

Howes, Virgil M., editor, *Individualizing Instruction.* New York: The Macmillan Company, 1970.

Howes, Virgil M., *Individualizing Instruction in Science and Mathematics.* New York: The Macmillan Company, 1970.

Kohl, Herbert R., *The Open Classroom.* New York: Random House, 1969.

Lewis, James, Jr., *Administering the Individualized Instruction Program.* West Nyack, New York:Parker Publishing Company, Inc., 1971.

Mager, Robert, S., *Preparing Instructional Objectives.* Palo Alto, California:Fearon Publications, 1967.

Palovic, Lora, and Goodman, Elizabeth, *The Elementary School Library in Action.* West Nyack, New York:Parker Publishing Company, Inc., 1968.

Scuorzo, Herbert, *Practical Audio-Visual Handbook for Teachers* West Nyack, New York:Parker Publishing Company, Inc., 1967.

Silberman, Charles E., *Crises in the Classroom.* New York:Random House, 1970.

Stahl, Dona and Anzalone, Patricia, *Individualized Teaching in the Elementary Schools.* West Nyack, New York:Parker Publishing Company, Inc., 1970.

Tanzman, Jack and Dunn, Kenneth J., *Using Instructional Media Effectively.* West Nyack, New York: Parker Publishing Company, Inc., 1971.

Weisgerber, Robert A., editor, *Developmental Efforts in Individualized Instruction.* Itasca, Illinois:Peacock Publishers, 1971.

Weisgerber, Robert A., editor, *Perspectives in Individualized Instruction.* Itasca, Illinois:Peacock Publishers, 1971.

Filmstrips:

"Individualization, Its Nature and Effects;" "Individualization, Its Objectives and Evaluative Procedures;" "Individualization, Its Materials and Their Use;" "Individualization, Diagnostic and Instructional Procedures;" "Individualization, Its Problems and Some Solutions." Washington, D.C.: National Education Association, Department of Audio-Visual Instruction, 1970.

INDEX